9/24/04
Susan Rautine

26 - blue & cream Columbine
[Colorado's state flower]
59 - ~~China~~ Tibet/?
61 - Kailas Range [see Circling the Sacred Mt.]
95 - pA young + woman gets rupees then loses field
whose produce is hers.

USMAN SHAH

AMONG THE TIBETANS

Isabella L. Bird

Illustrated by
Edward Whymper

DOVER PUBLICATIONS, INC.
Mineola, New York

Bibliographical Note

This Dover edition, first published in 2004, is an unabridged republication of the edition published by Fleming H. Revell Company, New York, in 1894.

Library of Congress Cataloging-in-Publication Data

Bird, Isabella L. (Isabella Lucy), 1831–1904.
    Among the Tibetans / Isabella L. Bird.
        p. cm.
    Originally published: New York : Religious Tract Society, 1894.
    ISBN 0-486-43435-4 (pbk.)
    1. Bird, Isabella L. (Isabella Lucy), 1831–1904—Travel—China—Tibet.
2. Tibet (China)—Description and travel. I. Title.

DS785.B62 2004
915.1'50435—dc22

2003064716

Manufactured in the United States of America
Dover Publications, Inc., 31 East 2nd Street, Mineola, N.Y. 11501

CONTENTS

—••—

LIST OF ILLUSTRATIONS

CHAPTER I

THE START

THE Vale of Kashmir is too well known to require
description. It is the 'happy hunting-ground' of the
Anglo-Indian sportsman and tourist, the resort of
artists and invalids, the home of *pashm* shawls and
exquisitely embroidered fabrics, and the land of Lalla
Rookh. Its inhabitants, chiefly Moslems, infamously
governed by Hindus, are a feeble race, attracting little
interest, valuable to travellers as 'coolies' or porters,
and repulsive to them from the mingled cunning and
obsequiousness which have been fostered by ages of
oppression. But even for them there is the dawn of
hope, for the Church Missionary Society has a strong
medical and educational mission at the capital,
a hospital and dispensary under the charge of a lady
M.D. have been opened for women, and a capable

and upright 'settlement officer,' lent by the Indian
Government, is investigating the iniquitous land
arrangements with a view to a just settlement.

I left the Panjāb railroad system at Rawul Pindi,
bought my camp equipage, and travelled through the
grand ravines which lead to Kashmir or the Jhelum
Valley by hill-cart, on horseback, and by house-boat,
reaching Srinagar at the end of April, when the velvet
lawns were at their greenest, and the foliage was at
its freshest, and the deodar-skirted mountains which
enclose this fairest gem of the Himalayas still wore
their winter mantle of unsullied snow.   Making Srinagar my headquarters, I spent two months in travelling
in Kashmir, half the time in a native house-boat
on the Jhelum and Pohru rivers, and the other half
on horseback, camping wherever the scenery was
most attractive.

By the middle of June mosquitos were rampant, the
grass was tawny, a brown dust haze hung over the
valley, the camp-fires of a multitude glared through
the hot nights and misty moonlight of the Munshibagh,
English tents dotted the landscape, there was no
mountain, valley, or plateau, however remote, free
from the clatter of English voices and the trained
servility of Hindu servants, and even Sonamarg, at
an altitude of 8,000 feet and rough of access, had

capitulated to lawn-tennis. To a traveller this Anglo-Indian hubbub was intolerable, and I left Srinagar and many kind friends on June 20 for the uplifted plateaux of Lesser Tibet. My party consisted of myself, a thoroughly competent servant and passable interpreter, Hassan Khan, a Panjābi; a *seis*, of whom the less that is said the better; and Mando, a Kashmiri lad, a common coolie, who, under Hassan Khan's training, developed into an efficient travelling servant, and later into a smart *khītmatgar*.

Gyalpo, my horse, must not be forgotten—indeed, he cannot be, for he left the marks of his heels or teeth on every one. He was a beautiful creature, Badakshani bred, of Arab blood, a silver-grey, as light as a greyhound and as strong as a cart-horse. He was higher in the scale of intellect than any horse of my acquaintance. His cleverness at times suggested reasoning power, and his mischievousness a sense of humour. He walked five miles an hour, jumped like a deer, climbed like a *yak*, was strong and steady in perilous fords, tireless, hardy, hungry, frolicked along ledges of precipices and over crevassed glaciers, was absolutely fearless, and his slender legs and the use he made of them were the marvel of all. He was an enigma to the end. He was quite untamable, rejected all dainties with indignation, swung his heels into

people's faces when they went near him, ran at them
with his teeth, seized unwary passers-by by their
kamar bands, and shook them as a dog shakes a rat,
would let no one go near him but Mando, for whom
he formed at first sight a most singular attachment,
but kicked and struck with his forefeet, his eyes all
the time dancing with fun, so that one could never
decide whether his ceaseless pranks were play or vice.
He was always tethered in front of my tent with a rope
twenty feet long, which left him practically free; he
was as good as a watchdog, and his antics and enig-
matical savagery were the life and terror of the camp.
I was never weary of watching him, the curves of his
form were so exquisite, his movements so lithe and
rapid, his small head and restless little ears so full of
life and expression, the variations in his manner so
frequent, one moment savagely attacking some unwary
stranger with a scream of rage, the next laying his
lovely head against Mando's cheek with a soft cooing
sound and a childlike gentleness. When he was
attacking anybody or frolicking, his movements and
beauty can only be described by a phrase of the
Apostle James, 'the grace of the fashion of it.'
Colonel Durand, of Gilgit celebrity, to whom I am
indebted for many other kindnesses, gave him to me
in exchange for a cowardly, heavy Yarkand horse, and

had previously vainly tried to tame him. His wild
eyes were like those of a seagull. He had no kinship
with humanity.

In addition, I had as escort an Afghan or Pathan,
a soldier of the Maharajah's irregular force of foreign
mercenaries, who had been sent to meet me when
I entered Kashmir. This man, Usman Shah, was
a stage ruffian in appearance. He wore a turban
of prodigious height ornamented with poppies or
birds' feathers, loved fantastic colours and ceaseless
change of raiment, walked in front of me carrying
a big sword over his shoulder, plundered and beat
the people, terrified the women, and was eventually
recognised at Leh as a murderer, and as great a
ruffian in reality as he was in appearance. An
attendant of this kind is a mistake. The brutality
and rapacity he exercises naturally make the people
cowardly or surly, and disinclined to trust a traveller
so accompanied.

Finally, I had a Cabul tent, 7 ft. 6 in. by 8 ft. 6 in.,
weighing, with poles and iron pins, 75 lbs., a trestle
bed and cork mattress, a folding table and chair,
and an Indian *dhurrie* as a carpet.

My servants had a tent 5 ft. 6 in. square, weighing
only 10 lbs., which served as a shelter tent for me
during the noonday halt. A kettle, copper pot, and

frying pan, a few enamelled iron table equipments, bedding, clothing, working and sketching materials, completed my outfit. The servants carried wadded quilts for beds and bedding, and their own cooking utensils, unwillingness to use those belonging to a Christian being nearly the last rag of religion which they retained. The only stores I carried were tea, a quantity of Edwards' desiccated soup, and a little saccharin. The 'house,' furniture, clothing, &c., were a light load for three mules, engaged at a shilling a day each, including the muleteer. Sheep, coarse flour, milk, and barley were procurable at very moderate prices on the road.

Leh, the capital of Ladakh or Lesser Tibet, is nineteen marches from Srinagar, but I occupied twenty-six days on the journey, and made the first 'march' by water, taking my house-boat to Ganderbal, a few hours from Srinagar, *viâ* the Mar Nullah and Anchar Lake. Never had this Venice of the Himalayas, with a broad rushing river for its high street and winding canals for its back streets, looked so entrancingly beautiful as in the slant sunshine of the late June afternoon. The light fell brightly on the river at the Residency stairs where I embarked, on *perindas* and state barges, with their painted arabesques, gay canopies, and 'banks' of

THE START FROM SRINAGAR

thirty and forty crimson-clad, blue-turbaned, paddling
men ; on the gay façade and gold-domed temple of
the Maharajah's Palace, on the massive deodar bridges
which for centuries have defied decay and the fierce
flood of the Jhelum, and on the quaintly picturesque
wooden architecture and carved brown lattice fronts
of the houses along the swirling waterway, and
glanced mirthfully through the dense leafage of the
superb planes which overhang the dark-green water.
But the mercury was 92° in the shade and the sunblaze terrific, and it was a relief when the boat
swung round a corner, and left the stir of the broad,
rapid Jhelum for a still, narrow, and sharply winding
canal, which intersects a part of Srinagar lying between the Jhelum and the hill-crowning fort of Hari
Parbat. There the shadows were deep, and chance
lights alone fell on the red dresses of the women
at the ghats, and on the shaven, shiny heads of
hundreds of amphibious boys who were swimming
and aquatically romping in the canal, which is at
once the sewer and the water supply of the district.

Several hours were spent in a slow and tortuous
progress through scenes of indescribable picturesqueness—a narrow waterway spanned by sharp-angled
stone bridges, some of them with houses on the top,
or by old brown wooden bridges festooned with vines,

hemmed in by lofty stone embankments into which sculptured stones from ancient temples are wrought, on the top of which are houses of rich men, fancifully built, with windows of fretwork of wood, or gardens with kiosks, and lower embankments sustaining many-balconied dwellings, rich in colour and fantastic in design, their upper fronts projecting over the water and supported on piles. There were gigantic poplars wreathed with vines, great mulberry trees hanging their tempting fruit just out of reach, huge planes overarching the water, their dense leafage scraping the mat roof of the boat; filthy ghats thronged with white-robed Moslems performing their scanty religious ablutions; great grain boats heavily thatched, containing not only families, but their sheep and poultry; and all the other sights of a crowded Srinagar waterway, the houses being characteristically distorted and out of repair. This canal gradually widens into the Anchar Lake, a reedy mere of indefinite boundaries, the breeding-ground of legions of mosquitos; and after the tawny twilight darkened into a stifling night we made fast to a reed bed, not reaching Ganderbal till late the next morning, where my horse and caravan awaited me under a splendid plane-tree.

For the next five days we marched up the Sind

CAMP AT GAGANGAIR

Valley, one of the most beautiful in Kashmir from its grandeur and variety. Beginning among quiet rice-fields and brown agricultural villages at an altitude of 5,000 feet, the track, usually bad and sometimes steep and perilous, passes through flower-gemmed alpine meadows, along dark gorges above the booming and rushing Sind, through woods matted with the sweet white jasmine, the lower hem of the pine and deodar forests which ascend the mountains to a considerable altitude, past rifts giving glimpses of dazzling snow-peaks, over grassy slopes dotted with villages, houses, and shrines embosomed in walnut groves, in sight of the frowning crags of Haramuk, through wooded lanes and park-like country over which farms are thinly scattered, over unrailed and shaky bridges, and across avalanche slopes, till it reaches Gagangair, a dream of lonely beauty, with a camping-ground of velvety sward under noble plane-trees. Above this place the valley closes in between walls of precipices and crags, which rise almost abruptly from the Sind to heights of 8,000 and 10,000 feet. The road in many places is only a series of steep and shelving ledges above the raging river, natural rock smoothed and polished into riskiness by the passage for centuries of the trade into Central Asia from Western India, Kashmir, and Afghanistan. Its precariousness for animals was emphasised to me by five serious accidents which occurred in the week of my journey, one of them involving the loss of the money, clothing, and sporting kit of an English officer bound for Ladakh for three months. Above this tremendous gorge the mountains open out, and after crossing to the left bank of the Sind a sharp ascent brought me to the beautiful alpine meadow of Sonamarg, bright with spring flowers, gleaming with crystal streams, and fringed on all sides by deciduous and coniferous trees, above and among which are great glaciers and the snowy peaks of Tilail. Fashion has deserted Sonamarg, rough of access, for Gulmarg, a caprice indicated by the ruins of several huts and of a church. The pure bracing air, magnificent views, the proximity and accessibility of glaciers, and the presence of a kind friend who was 'hutted' there for the summer, made Sonamarg a very pleasant halt before entering upon the supposed severities of the journey to Lesser Tibet.

The five days' march, though propitious and full of the charm of magnificent scenery, had opened my eyes to certain unpleasantnesses. I found that Usman Shah maltreated the villagers, and not only robbed them of their best fowls, but requisitioned

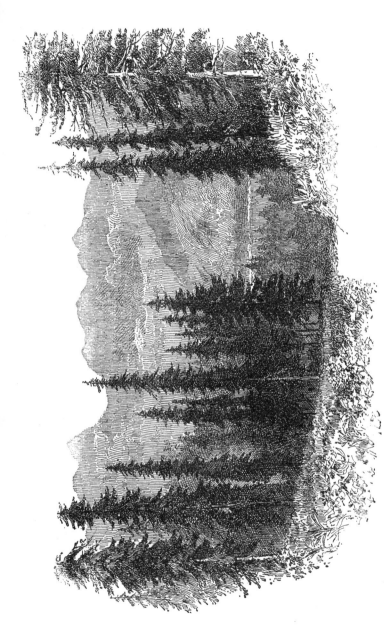

SONAMARG

all manner of things in my name, though I scrupulously and personally paid for everything, beating
the people with his scabbarded sword if they showed
any intention of standing upon their rights. Then
I found that my clever factotum, not content with the
legitimate 'squeeze' of ten per cent., was charging me
double price for everything and paying the sellers
only half the actual price, this legerdemain being
perpetrated in my presence. He also by threats got
back from the coolies half their day's wages after
I had paid them, received money for barley for Gyalpo,
and never bought it, a fact brought to light by the
growing feebleness of the horse, and cheated in all
sorts of mean and plausible ways, though I paid
him exceptionally high wages, and was prepared to
'wink' at a moderate amount of dishonesty, so long
as it affected only myself. It has a lowering influence
upon one to live in a fog of lies and fraud, and the
attempt to checkmate a fraudulent Asiatic ends in
extreme discomfiture.

I left Sonamarg late on a lovely afternoon for
a short march through forest-skirted alpine meadows
to Baltal, the last camping-ground in Kashmir, a
grassy valley at the foot of the Zoji La, the first of
three gigantic steps by which the lofty plateaux of
Central Asia are attained. On the road a large

affluent of the Sind, which tumbles down a pine-hung gorge in broad sheets of foam, has to be crossed. My *seis*, a rogue, was either half-witted or pretended to be so, and, in spite of orders to the contrary, led Gyalpo upon a bridge at a considerable height, formed of two poles with flat pieces of stone laid loosely over them not more than a foot broad. As the horse reached the middle, the structure gave a sort of turn, there was a vision of hoofs in air and a gleam of scarlet, and Gyalpo, the hope of the next four months, after rolling over more than once, vanished among rocks and surges of the wildest description. He kept his presence of mind, however, recovered himself, and by a desperate effort got ashore lower down, with legs scratched and bleeding and one horn of the saddle incurably bent.

Mr. Maconochie of the Panjāb Civil Service, and Dr. E. Neve of the C. M. S. Medical Mission in Kashmir, accompanied me from Sonamarg over the pass, and that night Mr. M. talked seriously to Usman Shah on the subject of his misconduct, and with such singular results that thereafter I had little cause for complaint. He came to me and said, 'The Commissioner Sahib thinks I give Mem Sahib a great deal of trouble;' to which I replied in a cold tone, 'Take care you don't give me any more.' The gist of the

Sahib's words was the very pertinent suggestion that it would eventually be more to his interest to serve me honestly and faithfully than to cheat me.

Baltal lies at the feet of a precipitous range, the peaks of which exceed Mont Blanc in height. Two gorges unite there. There is not a hut within ten miles. Big camp-fires blazed. A few shepherds lay under the shelter of a mat screen. The silence and solitude were most impressive under the frosty stars and the great Central Asian barrier. Sunrise the following morning saw us on the way up a huge gorge with nearly perpendicular sides, and filled to a great depth with snow. Then came the Zoji La, which, with the Namika La and the Fotu La, respectively 11,300, 13,000, and 13.500 feet, are the three great steps from Kashmir to the Tibetan heights. The two latter passes present no difficulties. The Zoji La is a thoroughly severe pass, the worst, with the exception perhaps of the Sasir, on the Yarkand caravan route. The track, cut, broken, and worn on the side of a wall of rock nearly 2,000 feet in abrupt elevation, is a series of rough narrow zigzags, rarely, if ever, wide enough for laden animals to pass each other, composed of broken ledges often nearly breast high, and shelving surfaces of abraded rock, up which animals have to leap and scramble as best they may.

Trees and trailers drooped over the path, ferns and lilies bloomed in moist recesses, and among myriads of flowers a large blue and cream columbine was conspicuous by its beauty and exquisite odour. The charm of the detail tempted one to linger at every turn, and all the more so because I knew that I should see nothing more of the grace and bounteousness of Nature till my projected descent into Kulu in the late autumn. The snow-filled gorge on whose abrupt side the path hangs, the Zoji La (Pass), is geographically remarkable as being the lowest depression in the great Himalayan range for 300 miles; and by it, in spite of infamous bits of road on the Sind and Suru rivers, and consequent losses of goods and animals, all the traffic of Kashmir, Afghanistan, and the Western Panjāb finds its way into Central Asia. It was too early in the season, however, for more than a few enterprising caravans to be on the road.

The last look upon Kashmir was a lingering one. Below, in shadow, lay the Baltal camping-ground, a lonely deodar-belted flowery meadow, noisy with the dash of icy torrents tumbling down from the snowfields and glaciers upborne by the gigantic mountain range into which we had penetrated by the Zoji Pass. The valley, lying in shadow at their base, was a dream of beauty, green as an English lawn,

starred with white lilies, and dotted with clumps of
trees which were festooned with red and white roses,
clematis, and white jasmine. Above the hardier
deciduous trees appeared the *Pinus excelsa*, the silver
fir, and the spruce; higher yet the stately grace of the
deodar clothed the hillsides; and above the forests
rose the snow mountains of Tilail, pink in the sunrise.
High above the Zoji, itself 11,500 feet in altitude,
a mass of grey and red mountains, snow-slashed and
snow-capped, rose in the dewy rose-flushed atmosphere
in peaks, walls, pinnacles, and jagged ridges, above
which towered yet loftier summits, bearing into the
heavenly blue sky fields of unsullied snow alone.
The descent on the Tibetan side is slight and gradual.
The character of the scenery undergoes an abrupt
change. There are no more trees, and the large
shrubs which for a time take their place degenerate
into thorny bushes, and then disappear. There were
mountains thinly clothed with grass here and there,
mountains of bare gravel and red rock, grey crags,
stretches of green turf, sunlit peaks with their snows,
a deep, snow-filled ravine, eastwards and beyond
a long valley filled with a snowfield fringed with pink
primulas; and that was CENTRAL ASIA.

We halted for breakfast, iced our cold tea in the
snow, Mr. M. gave a final charge to the Afghan,

who swore by his Prophet to be faithful, and I parted
from my kind escorts with much reluctance, and
started on my Tibetan journey, with but a slender
stock of Hindustani, and two men who spoke not
a word of English.   On that day's march of fourteen
miles there is not a single hut.   The snowfield
extended for five miles, from ten to seventy feet
deep, much crevassed, and encumbered with avalanches.   In it the Dras, truly 'snow-born,' appeared,
issuing from a chasm under a blue arch of ice and
snow, afterwards to rage down the valley, to be
forded many times or crossed on snow bridges.   After
walking for some time, and getting a bad fall down
an avalanche slope, I mounted Gyalpo, and the clever,
plucky fellow frolicked over the snow, smelt and
leapt crevasses which were too wide to be stepped
over, put his forelegs together and slid down slopes
like a Swiss mule, and, though carried off his feet
in a ford by the fierce surges of the Dras, struggled
gamely to shore.   Steep grassy hills, and peaks with
gorges cleft by the thundering Dras, and stretches
of rolling grass succeeded each other.   Then came
a wide valley mostly covered with stones brought
down by torrents, a few plots of miserable barley
grown by irrigation, and among them two buildings
of round stones and mud, about six feet high, with

flat mud roofs, one of which might be called the
village, and the other the caravanserai. On the
village roof were stacks of twigs and of the dried
dung of animals, which is used for fuel, and the whole
female population, adult and juvenile, engaged in
picking wool. The people of this village of Matayan
are Kashmiris. As I had an hour to wait for my
tent, the women descended and sat in a circle round
me with a concentrated stare. They asked if I were
dumb, and why I wore no earrings or necklace, their
own persons being loaded with heavy ornaments.
They brought children afflicted with skin-diseases, and
asked for ointment, and on hearing that I was hurt
by a fall, seized on my limbs and shampooed them
energetically but not undexterously. I prefer their
sociability to the usual chilling aloofness of the people
of Kashmir.

The Serai consisted of several dark and dirty cells,
built round a blazing piece of sloping dust, the only
camping-ground, and under the entrance two plat-
forms of animated earth, on which my servants
cooked and slept. The next day was Sunday, sacred
to a halt; but there was no fodder for the animals,
and we were obliged to march to Dras, following,
where possible, the course of the river of that name,
which passes among highly-coloured and snow-

slashed mountains, except in places where it suddenly
finds itself pent between walls of flame-coloured or
black rock, not ten feet apart, through which it boils
and rages, forming gigantic pot-holes. With every
mile the surroundings became more markedly of the
Central Asian type. All day long a white, scintillating
sun blazes out of a deep blue, rainless, cloudless sky.
The air is exhilarating. The traveller is conscious of
daily-increasing energy and vitality. There are no
trees, and deep crimson roses along torrent beds are
the only shrubs. But for a brief fortnight in June,
which chanced to occur during my journey, the
valleys and lower slopes present a wonderful aspect
of beauty and joyousness. Rose and pale pink
primulas fringe the margin of the snow, the dainty
Pedicularis tubiflora covers moist spots with its
mantle of gold ; great yellow and white, and small
purple and white anemones, pink and white dianthus,
a very large myosotis, bringing the intense blue of
heaven down to earth, purple orchids by the water,
borage staining whole tracts deep blue, martagon
lilies, pale green lilies veined and spotted with brown,
yellow, orange, and purple vetches, painter's brush,
dwarf dandelions, white clover, filling the air with
fragrance, pink and cream asters, chrysanthemums,
lychnis, irises, gentian, artemisia, and a hundred

others, form the undergrowth of millions of tall Umbelliferae and Compositae, many of them peach-scented and mostly yellow. The wind is always strong, and the millions of bright corollas, drinking in the sunblaze which perfects all too soon their brief but passionate existence, rippled in broad waves of colour with an almost kaleidoscopic effect. About the eleventh march from Srinagar, at Kargil, a change for the worse occurs, and the remaining marches to the capital of Ladakh are over blazing gravel or surfaces of denuded rock, the singular *Caprifolia horrida*, with its dark-green mass of wavy ovate leaves on trailing stems, and its fair, white, anemone-like blossom, and the graceful *Clematis orientalis*, the only vegetation.

Crossing a raging affluent of the Dras by a bridge which swayed and shivered, the top of a steep hill offered a view of a great valley with branches sloping up into the ravines of a complexity of mountain ranges, from 18,000 to 21,000 feet in altitude, with glaciers at times descending as low as 11,000 feet in their hollows. In consequence of such possibilities of irrigation, the valley is green with irrigated grass and barley, and villages with flat roofs scattered among the crops, or perched on the spurs of flame-coloured mountains, give it a wild cheerfulness. These Dras villages are inhabited by hardy Dards and Baltis, short, jolly-looking, darker, and far less handsome than the Kashmiris; but, unlike them, they showed so much friendliness, as well as interest and curiosity, that I remained with them for two days, visiting their villages and seeing the ' sights' they had to show me, chiefly a great Sikh fort, a *yak* bull, the *zho*, a hybrid, the interiors of their houses, a magnificent view from a hilltop, and a Dard dance to the music of Dard reed pipes. In return I sketched them individually and collectively as far as time allowed, presenting them with the results, truthful and ugly. I bought a sheep for 2s. 3d., and regaled the camp upon it, the three which were brought for my inspection being ridden by boys astride.

The evenings in the Dras valley were exquisite. As soon as the sun went behind the higher mountains, peak above peak, red and snow-slashed, flamed against a lemon sky, the strong wind moderated into a pure stiff breeze, bringing up to camp the thunder of the Dras, and the musical tinkle of streams sparkling in absolute purity. There was no more need for boiling and filtering. Icy water could be drunk in safety from every crystal torrent.

Leaving behind the Dras villages and their fertility,

the narrow road passes through a flaming valley above the Dras, walled in by bare, riven, snow-patched peaks, with steep declivities of stones, huge boulders, decaying avalanches, walls and spires of rock, some vermilion, others pink, a few intense orange, some black, and many plum-coloured, with a vitrified look, only to be represented by purple madder. Huge red chasms with glacier-fed torrents, occasional snowfields, intense solar heat radiating from dry and verdureless rock, a ravine so steep and narrow that for miles together there is not space to pitch a five-foot tent, the deafening roar of a river gathering volume and fury as it goes, rare openings, where willows are planted with lucerne in their irrigated shade, among which the traveller camps at night, and over all a sky of pure, intense blue purpling into starry night, were the features of the next three marches, noteworthy chiefly for the ex-change of the thundering Dras for the thundering Suru, and for some bad bridges and infamous bits of road before reaching Kargil, where the mountains swing apart, giving space to several villages. Miles of alluvium are under irrigation there, poplars, willows, and apricots abound, and on some damp sward under their shade at a great height I halted for two days to enjoy the magnificence of the scenery

and the refreshment of the greenery. These Kargil
villages are the capital of the small State of Purik,
under the Governorship of Baltistan or Little Tibet,
and are chiefly inhabited by Ladakhis who have
become converts to Islam. Racial characteristics,
dress, and manners are everywhere effaced or toned
down by Mohammedanism, and the chilling aloofness
and haughty bearing of Islam were very pronounced
among these converts.

The daily routine of the journey was as follows :
By six a.m. I sent on a coolie carrying the small tent
and lunch basket to await me half-way. Before
seven I started myself, with Usman Shah in front
of me, leaving the servants to follow with the caravan.
On reaching the shelter tent I halted for two hours,
or till the caravan had got a good start after passing
me. At the end of the march I usually found the
tent pitched on irrigated ground, near a hamlet, the
headman of which provided milk, fuel, fodder, and
other necessaries at fixed prices. 'Afternoon tea'
was speedily prepared, and dinner, consisting of
roast meat and boiled rice, was ready two hours later.
After dinner I usually conversed with the headman on local interests, and was in bed soon after
eight. The servants and muleteers fed and talked
till nine, when the sound of their 'hubble-bubbles'

indicated that they were going to sleep, like most Orientals, with their heads closely covered with their wadded quilts. Before starting each morning the account was made out, and I paid the headman personally.

The vagaries of the Afghan soldier, when they were not a cause of annoyance, were a constant amusement, though his ceaseless changes of finery and the daily growth of his baggage awakened grave suspicions. The swashbuckler marched four miles an hour in front of me with a swinging military stride, a large scimitar in a heavily ornamented scabbard over his shoulder. Tanned socks and sandals, black or white leggings wound round from ankle to knee with broad bands of orange or scarlet serge, white cambric knickerbockers, a white cambric shirt, with a short white muslin frock with hanging sleeves and a leather girdle over it, a red-peaked cap with a dark-blue *pagri* wound round it, with one end hanging over his back, earrings, a necklace, bracelets, and a profusion of rings, were his ordinary costume; and in his girdle he wore a dirk and a revolver, and suspended from it a long tobacco pouch made of the furry skin of some animal, a large leather purse, and etceteras. As the days went on he blossomed into blue and white muslin with a scarlet sash, wore a gold embroidered peak and a huge white muslin turban, with much change of ornaments, and appeared frequently with a great bunch of poppies or a cluster of crimson roses surmounting all. His headgear was colossal. It and the head together must have been fully a third of his total height. He was a most fantastic object, and very observant and skilful in his attentions to me; but if I had known what I afterwards knew, I should have hesitated about taking these long lonely marches with him for my sole attendant. Between Hassan Khan and this Afghan violent hatred and jealousy existed.

I have mentioned roads, and my road as the great caravan route from Western India into Central Asia. This is a fitting time for an explanation. The traveller who aspires to reach the highlands of Tibet from Kashmir cannot be borne along in a carriage or hill-cart. For much of the way he is limited to a foot pace, and if he has regard to his horse he walks down all rugged and steep descents, which are many, and dismounts at most bridges. By 'roads' must be understood bridle-paths, worn by traffic alone across the gravelly valleys, but elsewhere constructed with great toil and expense, as Nature compels the road-maker to follow her lead, and carry his track along the narrow valleys, ravines, gorges, and chasms which she has marked out for him. For miles at a time this road has been blasted out of precipices from 1,000 feet to 3,000 feet in depth, and is merely a ledge above a raging torrent, the worst parts, chiefly those round rocky projections, being 'scaffolded,' i. e. poles are lodged horizontally among the crevices of the cliff, and the roadway of slabs, planks, and brushwood, or branches and sods, is laid loosely upon them. This track is always amply wide enough for a loaded beast, but in many places, when two caravans meet, the animals of one must give way and scramble up the mountain-side, where foothold is often perilous, and always difficult. In passing a caravan near Kargil my servant's horse was pushed over the precipice by a loaded mule and drowned in the Suru, and at another time my Afghan caused the loss of a baggage mule of a Leh caravan by driving it off the track. To scatter a caravan so as to allow me to pass in solitary dignity he regarded as one of his functions, and on one occasion, on a very dangerous part of the road, as he was driving heavily laden mules up the steep rocks above, to their imminent peril and the distraction of their drivers, I was obliged to strike up his sword with my alpenstock to emphasise my abhorrence of his violence. The bridges are unrailed, and many of them are made by placing two or more logs across the stream, laying twigs across, and covering these with sods, but often so scantily that the wild rush of the water is seen below. Primitive as these bridges are, they involve great expense and difficulty in the bringing of long poplar logs for great distances along narrow mountain tracks by coolie labour, fifty men being required for the average log. The Ladakhi roads are admirable as compared with those of Kashmir, and are being constantly improved under the supervision of H. B. M.'s Joint Commissioner in Leh.

Up to Kargil the scenery, though growing more Tibetan with every march, had exhibited at intervals some traces of natural verdure; but beyond, after leaving the Suru, there is not a green thing, and on the next march the road crosses a lofty, sandy plateau, on which the heat was terrible— blazing gravel and a blazing heaven, then fiery cliffs and scorched hillsides, then a deep ravine and the large village of Paskim (dominated by a fort-crowned rock), and some planted and irrigated acres; then a narrow ravine and magnificent scenery flaming with colour, which opens out after some miles on a burning chaos of rocks and sand, mountain-girdled, and on some remarkable dwellings on a steep slope, with religious buildings singularly painted. This is Shergol, the first village of Buddhists, and there I was 'among the Tibetans.'

CHAPTER II

THE chaos of rocks and sand, walled in by vermilion and orange mountains, on which the village of Shergol stands, offered no facilities for camping; but somehow the men managed to pitch my tent on a steep slope, where I had to place my trestle bed astride an irrigation channel, down which the water bubbled noisily, on its way to keep alive some miserable patches of barley. At Shergol and elsewhere fodder is so scarce that the grain is not cut, but pulled up by the roots.

The intensely human interest of the journey began at that point. Not greater is the contrast between the grassy slopes and deodar-clothed mountains of Kashmir and the flaming aridity of Lesser Tibet, than between the tall, dark, handsome natives of the one, with their statuesque and shrinking women, and the ugly, short, squat, yellow-skinned, flat-nosed, oblique-eyed, uncouth-looking people of the other.

The Kashmiris are false, cringing, and suspicious; the Tibetans truthful, independent, and friendly, one of the pleasantest of peoples. I 'took' to them at once at Shergol, and terribly faulty though their morals are in some respects, I found no reason to change my good opinion of them in the succeeding four months.

The headman or *go-pa* came to see me, introduced me to the objects of interest, which are a *gonpo*, or monastery, built into the rock, with a brightly coloured front, and three *chod-tens*, or relic-holders, painted blue, red, and yellow, and daubed with coarse arabesques and representations of deities, one having a striking resemblance to Mr. Gladstone. The houses are of mud, with flat roofs; but, being summer, many of them were roofless, the poplar rods which support the mud having been used for fuel. Conical stacks of the dried excreta of animals, the chief fuel of the country, adorned the roofs, but the general aspect was ruinous and poor. The people all invited me into their dark and dirty rooms, inhabited also by goats, offered tea and cheese, and felt my clothes. They looked the wildest of savages, but they are not. No house was so poor as not to have its 'family altar,' its shelf of wooden gods, and table of offerings. A religious atmosphere pervades Tibet, and gives it

a singular sense of novelty. Not only were there
chod-tens and a *gonpo* in this poor place, and family
altars, but prayer-wheels, i.e. wooden cylinders filled
with rolls of paper inscribed with prayers, revolving
on sticks, to be turned by passers-by, inscribed cotton
bannerets on poles planted in cairns, and on the roofs

A HAND PRAYER-CYLINDER

long sticks, to which strips of cotton bearing the
universal prayer, *Aum mani padne hun* (O jewel of
the lotus-flower), are attached. As these wave in the
wind the occupants of the house gain the merit of
repeating this sentence.

The remaining marches to Leh, the capital of Lesser
Tibet, were full of fascination and novelty. Everywhere the Tibetans were friendly and cordial. In
each village I was invited to the headman's house,
and taken by him to visit the chief inhabitants;
every traveller, lay and clerical, passed by with the
cheerful salutation *Tzu*, asked me where I came from
and whither I was going, wished me a good journey,
admired Gyalpo, and when he scaled rock ladders and
scrambled gamely through difficult torrents, cheered
him like Englishmen, the general jollity and cordiality
of manners contrasting cheerily with the chilling
aloofness of Moslems.

The irredeemable ugliness of the Tibetans produced
a deeper impression daily. It is grotesque, and is
heightened, not modified, by their costume and ornament. They have high cheekbones, broad flat noses
without visible bridges, small, dark, oblique eyes,
with heavy lids and imperceptible eyebrows, wide
mouths, full lips, thick, big, projecting ears, deformed
by great hoops, straight black hair nearly as coarse
as horsehair, and short, square, ungainly figures. The
faces of the men are smooth. The women seldom
exceed five feet in height, and a man is tall at five
feet four.

The male costume is a long, loose, woollen coat

with a girdle, trousers, under-garments, woollen leggings, and a cap with a turned-up point over each ear. The girdle is the depository of many things dear to a Tibetan—his purse, rude knife, heavy tinder-box, tobacco pouch, pipe, distaff, and sundry charms and amulets. In the capacious breast of his coat he carries wool for spinning—for he spins as he walks—balls of cold barley dough, and much besides. He wears his hair in a pigtail. The women wear short, big-sleeved jackets, shortish, full-plaited skirts, tight trousers a yard too long, the superfluous length forming folds above the ankle, a sheepskin with the fur outside hangs over the back, and on gala occasions a sort of drapery is worn over the usual dress. Felt or straw shoes and many heavy ornaments are worn by both sexes. Great *ears* of brocade, lined and edged with fur and attached to the hair, are worn by the women. Their hair is dressed once a month in many much-greased plaits, fastened together at the back by a long tassel. The head-dress is a strip of cloth or leather, sewn over with large turquoises, carbuncles, and silver ornaments. This hangs in a point over the brow, broadens over the top of the head, and tapers as it reaches the waist behind. The ambition of every Tibetan girl is centred in this singular headgear. Hoops in the ears, necklaces, amulets, clasps, bangles of brass or silver, and various implements stuck in the girdle and depending from it, complete a costume pre-eminent in ugliness. The

TIBETAN GIRL

Tibetans are dirty. They wash once a year, and, except for festivals, seldom change their clothes till

they begin to drop off. They are healthy and hardy,
even the women can carry weights of sixty pounds
over the passes; they attain extreme old age; their
voices are harsh and loud, and their laughter is noisy
and hearty.

After leaving Shergol the signs of Buddhism were
universal and imposing, and the same may be said of
the whole of the inhabited part of Lesser Tibet.
Colossal figures of Shakya Thubba (Buddha) are
carved on faces of rock, or in wood, stone, or gilded
copper sit on lotus thrones in endless calm near
villages of votaries. *Chod-tens* from twenty to
a hundred feet in height, dedicated to 'holy' men,
are scattered over elevated ground, or in imposing
avenues line the approaches to hamlets and *gonpos*.
There are also countless *manis*, dykes of stone from
six to sixteen feet in width and from twenty feet to
a fourth of a mile in length, roofed with flattish stones,
inscribed by the *lamas* (monks) with the phrase *Aum*,
&c., and purchased and deposited by those who wish
to obtain any special benefit from the gods, such as
a safe journey. Then there are prayer-mills, sometimes 150 in a row, which revolve easily by being
brushed by the hand of the passer-by, larger prayer-
cylinders which are turned by pulling ropes, and
others larger still by water-power. The finest of the

latter was in a temple overarching a perennial torrent, and was said to contain 20,000 repetitions of
the mystic phrase, the fee to the worshipper for each
revolution of the cylinder being from 1*d.* to 1*s.* 4*d.*,
according to his means or urgency.

The glory and pride of Ladak and Nubra are the
gonpos, of which the illustrations give a slight idea.
Their picturesqueness is absolutely enchanting. They
are vast irregular piles of fantastic buildings, almost
invariably crowning lofty isolated rocks or mountain
spurs, reached by steep, rude rock staircases, *chod-
tens* below and battlemented towers above, with
temples, domes, bridges over chasms, spires, and
scaffolded projections gleaming with gold, looking,
as at Lamayuru, the outgrowth of the rock itself.
The outer walls are usually whitewashed, and red,
yellow, and brown wooden buildings, broad bands
of red and blue on the whitewash, tridents, prayer-
mills, *yaks'* tails, and flags on poles give colour and
movement, while the jangle of cymbals, the ringing
of bells, the incessant beating of big drums and
gongs, and the braying at intervals of six-foot silver
horns, attest the ritualistic activities of the com-
munities within. The *gonpos* contain from two up
to three hundred *lamas*. These are not cloistered,
and their duties take them freely among the people,

with whom they are closely linked, a younger son
in every family being a monk. Every act in trade,
agriculture, and social life needs the sanction of
sacerdotalism, whatever exists of wealth is in the
gonpos, which also have a monopoly of learning, and
11,000 monks, linked with the people, yet ruling all
affairs of life and death and beyond death, are connected closely by education, tradition, and authority
with Lhassa.

Passing along faces of precipices and over waterless plateaux of blazing red gravel—' waste places,'
truly—the journey was cheered by the meeting of
red and yellow *lamas* in companies, each *lama*
twirling his prayer-cylinder, abbots, and *skushoks*
(the latter believed to be incarnations of Buddha)
with many retainers, or gay groups of priestly
students, intoning in harsh and high-pitched monotones, *Aum mani padne hun*. And so past fascinating monastic buildings, through crystal torrents
rushing over red rock, through flaming ravines, on
rock ledges by scaffolded paths, camping in the
afternoons near friendly villages on oases of irrigated
alluvium, and down the Wanla water by the steepest
and narrowest cleft ever used for traffic, I reached
the Indus, crossed it by a wooden bridge where
its broad, fierce current is narrowed by rocks to

a width of sixty-five feet, and entered Ladak proper. A picturesque fort guards the bridge, and there travellers inscribe their names and are reported to Leh. I camped at Khalsi, a mile higher, but returned to the bridge in the evening to sketch, if I could, the grim nudity and repulsive horror of the surrounding mountains, attended only by Usman Shah. A few months earlier, this ruffian was sent down from Leh with six other soldiers and an officer to guard the fort, where they became the terror of all who crossed the bridge by their outrageous levies of blackmail. My swashbuckler quarrelled with the officer over a disreputable affair, and one night stabbed him mortally, induced his six comrades to plunge their knives into the body, sewed it up in a blanket, and threw it into the Indus, which disgorged it a little lower down. The men were all arrested and marched to Srinagar, where Usman turned 'king's evidence.'

The remaining marches were alongside of the tremendous granite ranges which divide the Indus from its great tributary, the Shayok. Colossal scenery, desperate aridity, tremendous solar heat, and an atmosphere highly rarefied and of nearly intolerable dryness, were the chief characteristics. At these Tibetan altitudes, where the valleys exceed

11,000 feet, the sun's rays are even more powerful
than on the 'burning plains of India.' The day
wind, rising at 9 a.m., and only falling near sunset,
blows with great heat and force. The solar heat at
noon was from 120° to 130°, and at night the
mercury frequently fell below the freezing point.
I did not suffer from the climate, but in the case
of most Europeans the air passages become irritated,
the skin cracks, and after a time the action of the
heart is affected. The hair when released stands out
from the head, leather shrivels and splits, horn
combs break to pieces, food dries up, rapid evapora-
tion renders water-colour sketching nearly impossible,
and tea made with water from fifteen to twenty
below the boiling-point of 212 degrees, is flavourless
and flat.

After a delightful journey of twenty-five days
I camped at Spitak, among the *chod-tens* and *manis*
which cluster round the base of a lofty and isolated
rock, crowned with one of the most striking monasteries in Ladak, and very early the next morning,
under a sun of terrific fierceness, rode up a five-mile
slope of blazing gravel to the goal of my long march.
Even at a short distance off, the Tibetan capital
can scarcely be distinguished from the bare, ribbed,
scored, jagged, vermilion and rose-red mountains

GONPO OF SPITAK

which nearly surround it, were it not for the palace
of the former kings or Gyalpos of Ladak, a huge
building attaining ten storeys in height, with massive
walls sloping inwards, while long balconies and
galleries, carved projections of brown wood, and
prominent windows, give it a singular picturesqueness. It can be seen for many miles, and dwarfs
the little Central Asian town which clusters round
its base.

Long lines of *chod-tens* and *manis* mark the
approach to Leh. Then come barley fields and
poplar and willow plantations, bright streams are
crossed, and a small gateway, within which is
a colony of very poor Baltis, gives access to the
city. In consequence of ' the vigilance of the guard
at the bridge of Khalsi,' I was expected, and was
met at the gate by the wazir's *jemadar*, or head of
police, in artistic attire, with *spahis* in apricot
turbans, violet *chogas*, and green leggings, who
cleared the way with spears, Gyalpo frolicking as
merrily and as ready to bite, and the Afghan
striding in front as firmly, as though they had not
marched for twenty-five days through the rugged
passes of the Himalayas. In such wise I was
escorted to a shady bungalow of three rooms, in
the grounds of H. B. M.'s Joint Commissioner, who

lives at Leh during the four months of the 'caravan season,' to assist in regulating the traffic and to guard the interests of the numerous British subjects who pass through Leh with merchandise. For their benefit also, the Indian Government aids in the support of a small hospital, open, however, to all, which, with a largely attended dispensary, is under the charge of a Moravian medical missionary.

Just outside the Commissioner's grounds are two very humble whitewashed dwellings, with small gardens brilliant with European flowers; and in these the two Moravian missionaries, the only permanent European residents in Leh, were living, Mr. Redslob and Dr. Karl Marx, with their wives. Dr. Marx was at his gate to welcome me.

To these two men, especially the former, I owe a debt of gratitude which in no shape, not even by the hearty acknowledgment of it, can ever be repaid, for they died within a few days of each other, of an epidemic, last year, Dr. Marx and a new-born son being buried in one grave. For twenty-five years Mr. Redslob, a man of noble physique and intellect, a scholar and linguist, an expert botanist and an admirable artist, devoted himself to the welfare of the Tibetans, and though his great aim was to Christianize them, he gained their confidence so thoroughly by his virtues, kindness, profound Tibetan scholarship, and manliness, that he was loved and welcomed everywhere, and is now mourned for as the best and truest friend the people ever had.

I had scarcely finished breakfast when he called; a man of great height and strong voice, with a cheery manner, a face beaming with kindness, and speaking excellent English. Leh was the goal of my journey, but Mr. Redslob came with a proposal to escort me over the great passes to the northward for a three weeks' journey to Nubra, a district formed of the combined valleys of the Shayok and Nubra rivers, tributaries of the Indus, and abounding in interest. Of course I at once accepted an offer so full of advantages, and the performance was better even than the promise.

Two days were occupied in making preparations, but afterwards I spent a fortnight in my tent at Leh, a city by no means to be passed over without remark, for, though it and the region of which it is the capital are very remote from the thoughts of most readers, it is one of the centres of Central Asian commerce. There all traders from India, Kashmir, and Afghanistan must halt for animals and supplies on their way to Yarkand and Khotan, and there also merchants from the mysterious city of Lhassa do a great business in brick tea and in Lhassa wares, chiefly ecclesiastical.

The situation of Leh is a grand one, the great Kailas range, with its glaciers and snowfields, rising just behind it to the north, its passes alone reaching an altitude of nearly 18,000 feet; while to the south, across a gravelly descent and the Indus Valley, rise great red ranges dominated by snow-peaks exceeding 21,000 feet in altitude. The centre of Leh is a wide bazaar, where much polo is played in the afternoons; and above this the irregular, flat-roofed, many-balconied houses of the town cluster round the palace and a gigantic *chod-ten* alongside it. The rugged crest of the rock on a spur of which the palace stands is crowned by the fantastic buildings of an ancient *gonpo*. Beyond the crops and plantations which surround the town lies a flaming desert of gravel or rock. The architectural features of Leh, except of the palace, are mean. A new mosque glaring with vulgar colour, a treasury and court of justice, the wazir's bungalow, a Moslem cemetery, and Buddhist cremation grounds, in which each family has its separate burning place, are all that is noteworthy. The narrow alleys, which would be abominably dirty if dirt were possible in a climate of such intense dryness, house a very mixed population, in which the Moslem element is always

LEH

increasing, partly owing to the renewal of that prose-
lytising energy which is making itself felt throughout
Asia, and partly to the marriages of Moslem traders
with Ladaki women, who embrace the faith of their
husbands and bring up their families in the same.

On my arrival few of the shops in the great *place,*
or bazaar, were open, and there was no business; but
a few weeks later the little desert capital nearly
doubled its population, and during August the din
and stir of trade and amusements ceased not by day
or night, and the shifting scenes were as gay in
colouring and as full of variety as could be desired.

Great caravans *en route* for Khotan, Yarkand, and
even Chinese Tibet arrived daily from Kashmir, the
Panjāb, and Afghanistan, and stacked their bales of
goods in the *place*; the Lhassa traders opened shops
in which the specialties were brick tea and instruments of worship; merchants from Amritsar, Cabul,
Bokhara, and Yarkand, stately in costume and gait,
thronged the bazaar and opened bales of costly goods
in tantalising fashion; mules, asses, horses, and *yaks*
kicked, squealed, and bellowed; the dissonance of
bargaining tongues rose high; there were mendicant
monks, Indian fakirs, Moslem dervishes, Mecca pilgrims,
itinerant musicians, and Buddhist ballad howlers;
bold-faced women with creels on their backs brought

in lucerne; Ladakis, Baltis, and Lahulis tended the beasts, and the wazir's *jemadar* and gay *spahis* moved about among the throngs. In the midst of this picturesque confusion, the short, square-built, Lhassa traders, who face the blazing sun in heavy winter clothing, exchange their expensive tea for Nubra and Baltistan dried apricots, Kashmir saffron, and rich stuffs from India; and merchants from Yarkand on big Turkestan horses offer hemp, which is smoked as opium, and Russian trifles and dress goods, under cloudless skies. With the huge Kailas range as a background, this great rendezvous of Central Asian traffic has a great fascination, even though moral shadows of the darkest kind abound.

On the second morning, while I was taking the sketch of Usman Shah which appears as the frontispiece, he was recognised both by the Joint Commissioner and the chief of police as a mutineer and murderer, and was marched out of Leh. I was asked to look over my baggage, but did not. I had trusted him, he had been faithful in his way, and later I found that nothing was missing. He was a brutal ruffian, one of a band of irregulars sent by the Maharajah of Kashmir to garrison the fort at Leh. From it they used to descend on the town, plunder the bazaar, insult the women, take all they wanted without pay-

ment, and when one of their number was being tried
for some offence, they dragged the judge out of court
and beat him! After holding Leh in terror for some
time the British Commissioner obtained their removal.
It was, however, at the fort at the Indus bridge, as
related before, that the crime of murder was committed. Still there was something almost grand in
the defiant attitude of the fantastic swashbuckler,
as, standing outside the bungalow, he faced the British
Commissioner, to him the embodiment of all earthly
power, and the chief of police, and defied them. Not
an inch would he stir till the wazir gave him a coolie
to carry his baggage. He had been acquitted of the
murder, he said, 'and though I killed the man, it was
according to the custom of my country—he gave me
an insult which could only be wiped out in blood!'
The guard dared not touch him, and he went to the
wazir, demanded a coolie, and got one!

Our party left Leh early on a glorious morning,
travelling light, Mr. Redslob, a very learned Lhassa
monk, named Gergan, Mr. R.'s servant, my three, and
four baggage horses, with two drivers engaged for the
journey. The great Kailas range was to be crossed,
and the first day's march up long, barren, stony valleys,
without interest, took us to a piece of level ground,
with a small semi-subterranean refuge on which

there was barely room for two tents, at the altitude
of the summit of Mont Blanc. For two hours before
we reached it the men and animals showed great
distress. Gyalpo stopped every few yards, gasping,
with blood trickling from his nostrils, and turned his
head so as to look at me, with the question in his eyes,
What does this mean? Hassan Khan was reeling
from vertigo, but would not give in; the *seis*, a creature
without pluck, was carried in a blanket slung on my
tent poles, and even the Tibetans suffered. I felt no
inconvenience, but as I unsaddled Gyalpo I was glad
that there was no more work to do! This 'mountain-
sickness,' called by the natives *ladug*, or 'pass-poison,'
is supposed by them to be the result of the odour or
pollen of certain plants which grow on the passes.
Horses and mules are unable to carry their loads, and
men suffer from vertigo, vomiting, violent headache
and bleeding from the nose, mouth, and ears, as well
as prostration of strength, sometimes complete, and
occasionally ending fatally.

After a bitterly cold night I was awakened at dawn
by novel sounds, gruntings, and low, resonant bellowing round my tent, and the grey light revealed
several *yaks* (the *Bos grunniens*, the Tibetan ox), the
pride of the Tibetan highlands. This magnificent
animal, though not exceeding an English shorthorn

cow in height, looks gigantic, with his thick curved
horns, his wild eyes glaring from under a mass of
curls, his long thick hair hanging to his fetlocks, and
his huge bushy tail. He is usually black or tawny,
but the tail is often white, and is the length of his
long hair. The nose is fine and has a look of breeding
as well as power. He only flourishes at altitudes
exceeding 12,000 feet. Even after generations of
semi-domestication he is very wild, and can only be
managed by being led with a rope attached to a ring
in the nostrils. He disdains the plough, but conde-
scends to carry burdens, and numbers of the Ladak
and Nubra people get their living by carrying goods
for the traders on his broad back over the great passes.
His legs are very short, and he has a sensible way of
measuring distance with his eyes and planting his
feet, which enables him to carry loads where it might
be supposed that only a goat could climb. He picks
up a living anyhow, in that respect resembling the
camel.

He has an uncertain temper, and is not favourably
disposed towards his rider. Indeed, my experience
was that just as one was about to mount him he
usually made a lunge at one with his horns. Some
of my *yak* steeds shied, plunged, kicked, executed
fantastic movements on the ledges of precipices,

knocked down their leaders, bellowed defiance, and
rushed madly down mountain sides, leaping from
boulder to boulder, till they landed me among their
fellows. The rush of a herd of bellowing *yaks* at a
wild gallop, waving their huge tails, is a grand sight.

My first *yak* was fairly quiet, and looked a noble
steed, with my Mexican saddle and gay blanket
among rather than upon his thick black locks. His
back seemed as broad as that of an elephant, and
with his slow, sure, resolute step, he was like a
mountain in motion. We took five hours for the
ascent of the Digar Pass, our loads and some of us
on *yaks*, some walking, and those who suffered most
from the 'pass-poison' and could not sit on *yaks*
were carried. A number of Tibetans went up with
us. It was a new thing for a European lady to travel
in Nubra, and they took a friendly interest in my
getting through all right. The dreary stretches of
the ascent, though at first white with *edelweiss*, of
which the people make their tinder, are surmounted
for the most part by steep, short zigzags of broken
stone. The heavens were dark with snow-showers,
the wind was high and the cold severe, and gasping
horses, and men prostrate on their faces unable to
move, suggested a considerable amount of suffering;
but all safely reached the summit, 17,930 feet,

where in a snowstorm the guides huzzaed, praised
their gods, and tucked rag streamers into a cairn.
The loads were replaced on the horses, and over
wastes of ice, across snowfields margined by broad
splashes of rose-red primulas, down desert valleys
and along irrigated hillsides, we descended 3,700
feet to the village of Digar in Nubra, where under
a cloudless sky the mercury stood at 90°!

Upper and Lower Nubra consist of the valleys of
the Nubra and Shayok rivers. These are deep,
fierce, variable streams, which have buried the lower
levels under great stretches of shingle, patched with
jungles of *hippophaë* and tamarisk, affording cover
for innumerable wolves. Great lateral torrents descend to these rivers, and on alluvial ridges formed
at the junctions are the villages with their pleasant
surroundings of barley, lucerne, wheat, with poplar
and fruit trees, and their picturesque *gonpos* crowning spurs of rock above them. The first view of
Nubra is not beautiful. Yellow, absolutely barren
mountains, cleft by yellow gorges, and apparently
formed of yellow gravel, the huge rifts in their sides
alone showing their substructure of rock, look as if
they had never been finished, or had been finished
so long that they had returned to chaos. These
hem in a valley of grey sand and shingle, threaded

by a greyish stream. From the second view point
mountains are seen descending on a pleasanter part
of the Shayok valley in grey, yellow, or vermilion
masses of naked rock, 7,000 and 8,000 feet in height,

A CHOD-TEN

above which rise snow-capped peaks sending out fantastic spurs and buttresses, while the colossal walls
of rock are cleft by rifts as colossal. The central

ridge between the Nubra and Upper Shayok valleys is 20,000 feet in altitude, and on this are super-imposed five peaks of rock, ascertained by survey to be from 24,000 to 25,000 feet in height, while at one point the eye takes in a nearly vertical height of 14,000 feet from the level of the Shayok River! The Shayok and Nubra valleys are only five and four miles in width respectively at their widest parts. The early winter traffic chiefly follows along river beds, then nearly dry, while summer caravans have to labour along difficult tracks at great heights, where mud and snow avalanches are common, to climb dangerous rock ladders, and to cross glaciers and the risky fords of the Shayok. Nubra is similar in character to Ladak, but it is hotter and more fertile, the mountains are loftier, the *gonpos* are more nu-merous, and the people are simpler, more religious, and more purely Tibetan. Mr. Redslob loved Nubra, and as love begets love he received a hearty welcome at Digar and everywhere else.

The descent to the Shayok River gave us a most severe day of twelve hours. The river had covered the usual track, and we had to take to torrent beds and precipice ledges, I on one *yak*, and my tent on another. In years of travel I have never seen such difficulties. Eventually at dusk Mr. Redslob, Gergan, the servants, and I descended on a broad shingle bed by the rushing Shayok ; but it was not till dawn on the following day that, by means of our two *yaks* and the muleteers, our baggage and food arrived, the baggage horses being brought down unloaded, with men holding the head and tail of each. Our saddle horses, which we led with us, were much cut by falls. Gyalpo fell fully twenty feet, and got his side laid open. The baggage horses, according to their owners, had all gone over one precipice, which delayed them five hours.

Below us lay two leaky scows, and eight men from Sati, on the other side of the Shayok, are pledged to the Government to ferry travellers ; but no amount of shouting and yelling, or burning of brushwood, or even firing, brought them to the rescue, though their pleasant lights were only a mile off. Snow fell, the wind was strong and keen, and our tent-pegs were only kept down by heavy stones. Blankets in abundance were laid down, yet failed to soften the ' paving stones ' on which I slept that night ! We had tea and rice, but our men, whose baggage was astray on the mountains, were without food for twenty-two hours, positively refusing to eat our food or cook fresh rice in our cooking pots ! To such an extent has Hindu caste-feeling infected Moslems !

The disasters of that day's march, besides various breakages, were, two servants helpless from 'pass-poison' and bruises; a Ladaki, who had rolled over a precipice, with a broken arm, and Gergan bleeding from an ugly scalp wound, also from a fall.

By eight o'clock the next morning the sun was high and brilliant, the snows of the ravines under its fierce heat were melting fast, and the river, roaring hoarsely, was a mad rush of grey rapids and grey foam; but three weeks later in the season, lower down, its many branches are only two feet deep. This Shayok, which cannot in any way be circumvented, is the great obstacle on this Yarkand trade route. Travellers and their goods make the perilous passage in the scow, but their animals swim, and are often paralysed by the ice-cold water and drowned. My Moslem servants, white-lipped and trembling, committed themselves to Allah on the river bank, and the Buddhists worshipped their sleeve idols. The *gopa*, or headman of Sati, a splendid fellow, who accompanied us through Nubra, and eight wild-looking, half-naked satellites, were the Charons of that Styx. They poled and paddled with yells of excitement; the rapids seized the scow, and carried her broadside down into hissing and raging surges; then there was a plash, a leap of maddened water half filling the boat,

a struggle, a whirl, violent efforts, and a united yell,
and far down the torrent we were in smooth water
on the opposite shore. The ferrymen recrossed, pulled
our saddle horses by ropes into the river, the *gopa*
held them ; again the scow and her frantic crew,
poling, paddling, and yelling, were hurried broadside
down, and as they swept past there were glimpses
above and among the foam-crested surges of the
wild-looking heads and drifting forelocks of two
grey horses swimming desperately for their lives,—
a splendid sight. They landed safely, but of the
baggage animals one was sucked under the boat and
drowned, and as the others refused to face the rapids,
we had to obtain other transport. A few days later
the scow, which was brought up in pieces from
Kashmir on coolies' backs at a cost of four hundred
rupees, was dashed to pieces !

A halt for Sunday in an apricot grove in the
pleasant village of Sati refreshed us all for the long
marches which followed, by which we crossed the
Sasir Pass, full of difficulties from snow and glaciers,
which extend for many miles, to the Dipsang Plain,
the bleakest and dreariest of Central Asian wastes,
from which the gentle ascent of the Karakorum Pass
rises, and returned, varying our route slightly, to the
pleasant villages of the Nubra valley. Everywhere

Mr. Redslob's Tibetan scholarship, his old-world courtesy, his kindness and adaptability, and his medical skill, ensured us a welcome the heartiness of which I cannot describe. The headmen and elders of the villages came to meet us when we arrived, and escorted us when we left; the monasteries and houses with the best they contained were thrown open to us; the men sat round our camp-fires at night, telling stories and local gossip, and asking questions, everything being translated to me by my kind guide, and so we actually lived 'among the Tibetans.'

CHAPTER III

NUBRA

In order to visit Lower Nubra and return to Leh we were obliged to cross the great fords of the Shayok at the most dangerous season of the year. This transit had been the bugbear of the journey ever since news reached us of the destruction of the Sati scow. Mr. Redslob questioned every man we met on the subject, solemn and noisy conclaves were held upon it round the camp-fires, it was said that the 'European woman' and her 'spider-legged horse' could never get across, and for days before we reached the stream, the *chupas*, or government water-guides, made nightly reports to the village headmen of the state of the waters, which were steadily rising, the final verdict being that they were only just practicable for strong horses. To delay till the waters fell was impossible. Mr. Redslob had engagements in Leh, and I was already somewhat late for the passage of the lofty passes between Tibet and British

India before the winter, so we decided on crossing with every precaution which experience could suggest.

At Lagshung, the evening before, the Tibetans made prayers and offerings for a day cloudy enough to keep the water down, but in the morning from a cloudless sky a scintillating sun blazed down like a magnesium light, and every glacier and snowfield sent its tribute torrent to the Shayok. In crossing a stretch of white sand the solar heat was so fierce that our European skins were blistered through our clothing. We halted at Lagshung, at the house of a friendly *zemindar*, who pressed upon me the loan of a big Yarkand horse for the ford, a kindness which nearly proved fatal; and then by shingle paths through lacerating thickets of the horrid *Hippophaë rhamnoides*, we reached a *chod-ten* on the shingly bank of the river, where the Tibetans renewed their prayers and offerings, and the final orders for the crossing were issued. We had twelve horses, carrying only quarter loads each, all led; the servants were mounted, 'water-guides' with ten-foot poles sounded the river ahead, one led Mr. Redslob's horse (the rider being bare-legged) in front of mine with a long rope, and two more led mine, while the *gopas* of three villages and the *zemindar* steadied my horse against the stream. The water-guides only wore girdles, and with elf-locks and pigtails streaming from their heads, and their uncouth yells and wild gesticulations, they looked true river-demons.

A LAMA

The Shayok presented an expanse of eight branches and a main stream, divided by shallows and shingle

banks, the whole a mile and a half in width. On the
brink the *chupas* made us all drink good draughts of
the turbid river water, ' to prevent giddiness,' they
said, and they added that I must not think them rude
if they dashed water at my face frequently with the
same object. Hassan Khan, and Mando, who was livid
with fright, wore dark-green goggles, that they might
not see the rapids. In the second branch the water
reached the horses' bodies, and my animal tottered
and swerved. There were bursts of wild laughter,
not merriment but excitement, accompanied by yells
as the streams grew fiercer, a loud chorus of *Kabadar!
Sharbaz!* ('Caution!' 'Well done!') was yelled to
encourage the horses, and the boom and hiss of the
Shayok made a wild accompaniment. Gyalpo, for
whose legs of steel I longed, frolicked as usual, making
mirthful lunges at his leader when the pair halted.
Hassan Khan, in the deepest branch, shakily said to
me, ' I not afraid, Mem Sahib.' During the hour spent
in crossing the eight branches, I thought that the risk
had been exaggerated, and that giddiness was the
chief peril.

But when we halted, cold and dripping, on the
shingle bank of the main stream I changed my
mind. A deep, fierce, swirling rapid, with a calmer
depth below its farther bank, and fully a quarter of

a mile wide, was yet to be crossed.   The business was
serious.   All the *chupas* went up and down, sounding,
long before they found a possible passage.   All loads
were raised higher, the men roped their soaked clothing on their shoulders, water was dashed repeatedly
at our faces, girths were tightened, and then, with
shouts and yells, the whole caravan plunged into deep
water, strong, and almost ice-cold.   Half an hour was
spent in that devious ford, without any apparent
progress, for in the dizzy swirl the horses simply
seemed treading the water backwards.   Louder grew
the yells as the torrent raged more hoarsely, the
chorus of *kabadar* grew frantic, the water was up to
the men's armpits and the seat of my saddle, my horse
tottered and swerved several times, the nearing shore
presented an abrupt bank underscooped by the stream.
There was a deeper plunge, an encouraging shout, and
Mr. Redslob's strong horse leapt the bank.   The *gopas*
encouraged mine; he made a desperate effort, but fell
short and rolled over backwards into the Shayok with
his rider under him.   A struggle, a moment of suffo-
cation, and I was extricated by strong arms, to be
knocked down again by the rush of the water, to be
again dragged up and hauled and hoisted up the
crumbling bank.   I escaped with a broken rib and
some severe bruises, but the horse was drowned.

Mr. Redslob, who had thought that my life could not be saved, and the Tibetans were so distressed by the

THREE GOPAS

accident that I made very light of it, and only took one day of rest. The following morning some men

and animals were carried away, and afterwards the
ford was impassable for a fortnight. Such risks are
among the amenities of the great trade route from
India into Central Asia !

The Lower Nubra valley is wilder and narrower
than the Upper, its apricot orchards more luxuriant,
its wolf-haunted *hippophaë* and tamarisk thickets more
dense. Its villages are always close to ravines, the
mouths of which are filled with *chod-tens, manis,*
prayer-wheels, and religious buildings. Access to
them is usually up the stony beds of streams over-
arched by apricots. The camping-grounds are apricot
orchards. The apricot foliage is rich, and the fruit
small but delicious. The largest fruit tree I saw
measured nine feet six inches in girth six feet from
the ground. Strangers are welcome to eat as much
of the fruit as they please, provided that they return
the stones to the proprietor. It is true that Nubra
exports dried apricots, and the women were splitting
and drying the fruit on every house roof, but the
special *raison d'être* of the tree is the clear, white,
fragrant, and highly illuminating oil made from the
kernels by the simple process of crushing them between two stones. In every *gonpo* temple a silver
bowl holding from four to six gallons is replenished
annually with this almond-scented oil for the ever-

burning light before the shrine of Buddha. It is used for lamps, and very largely in cookery. Children, instead of being washed, are rubbed daily with it, and on being weaned at the age of four or five, are fed for some time, or rather crammed, with balls of barley-meal made into a paste with it.

At Hundar, a superbly situated village, which we visited twice, we were received at the house of Gergan the monk, who had accompanied us throughout. He is a *zemindar*, and the large house in which he made us welcome stands in his own patrimony. Everything was prepared for us. The mud floors were swept, cotton quilts were laid down on the balconies, blue cornflowers and marigolds, cultivated for religious ornament, were in all the rooms, and the women were in gala dress and loaded with coarse jewellery. Right hearty was the welcome. Mr. Redslob loved, and therefore was loved. The Tibetans to him were not 'natives,' but brothers. He drew the best out of them. Their superstitions and beliefs were not to him 'rubbish,' but subjects for minute investigation and study. His courtesy to all was frank and dignified. In his dealings he was scrupulously just. He was intensely interested in their interests. His Tibetan scholarship and knowledge of Tibetan sacred literature gave him almost the standing of an abbot among them, and his medical skill and knowledge, joyfully used for their benefit on former occasions, had won their regard. So at Hundar, as everywhere else, the elders came out to meet us and cut the apricot branches away on our road, and the silver horns of the *gonpo* above brayed a dissonant welcome. Along the Indus valley the servants of Englishmen beat the Tibetans, in the Shayok and Nubra valleys the Yarkand traders beat and cheat them, and the women are shy with strangers, but at Hundar they were frank and friendly with me, saying, as many others had said, ' We will trust any one who comes with the missionary.'

Gergan's home was typical of the dwellings of the richer cultivators and landholders. It was a large, rambling, three-storeyed house, the lower part of stone, the upper of huge sun-dried bricks. It was adorned with projecting windows and brown wooden balconies. Fuel—the dried excreta of animals—is too scarce to be used for any but cooking purposes, and on these balconies in the severe cold of winter the people sit to imbibe the warm sunshine. The rooms were large, ceiled with peeled poplar rods, and floored with split white pebbles set in clay. There was a temple on the roof, and in it, on a platform, were life-size images of Buddha, seated in eternal calm, with his downcast eyes and mild Hindu face, the thousand-armed Chan-ra-zigs (the great Mercy), Jam-pal-yangs (the Wisdom), and Chag-na-dorje (the Justice). In front on a table or altar were seven small lamps, burning apricot oil, and twenty small brass cups, containing minute offerings of rice and other things, changed daily. There were prayer-wheels, cymbals, horns and drums, and a prayer-cylinder six feet high, which it took the strength of two men to turn. On a shelf immediately below the idols were the brazen sceptre, bell, and thunderbolt, a brass lotus blossom, and the spouted brass flagon decorated with peacocks' feathers, which is used at baptisms, and for pouring holy water upon the hands at festivals. In houses in which there is not a roof temple the best room is set apart for religious use and for these divinities, which are always surrounded with musical instruments and symbols of power, and receive worship and offerings daily, Tibetan Buddhism being a religion of the family and household. In his family temple Gergan offered gifts and thanks for the deliverances of the journey. He had been assisting Mr. Redslob for two years in the translation of the New Testament, and had wept over the love and sufferings of our Lord Jesus Christ. He had even desired that his son should receive baptism and be brought up as a Christian, but for himself he 'could not break with custom and his ancestral creed.'

In the usual living-room of the family a platform, raised only a few inches, ran partly round the wall. In the middle of the floor there was a clay fireplace, with a prayer-wheel and some clay and brass cooking pots upon it. A few shelves, fire-bars for roasting barley, a wooden churn, and some spinning arrangements were the furniture. A number of small dark rooms used for sleeping and storage opened from this, and above were the balconies and reception rooms. Wooden posts supported the roofs, and these were wreathed with lucerne, the firstfruits of the field. Narrow, steep staircases in all Tibetan houses lead to the family rooms. In winter the people live below, alongside of the animals and fodder. In summer they sleep in loosely built booths of poplar branches on the roof. Gergan's roof was covered, like others at the time, to the depth of two feet, with hay, i. e. grass and lucerne, which are wound into long ropes, experience having taught the Tibetans that their scarce fodder is best preserved thus from breakage and waste. I bought hay by the yard for Gyalpo.

Our food in this hospitable house was simple— apricots, fresh, or dried and stewed with honey; *zho's* milk, curds and cheese, sour cream, peas, beans, balls

of barley dough, barley porridge, and 'broth of
abominable things.' *Chang*, a dirty-looking beer
made from barley, was offered with each meal, and
tea frequently, but I took my own 'on the sly.' I
have mentioned a churn as part of the 'plenishings'
of the living-room. In Tibet the churn is used for
making tea! I give the recipe. 'For six persons.
Boil a teacupful of tea in three pints of water for ten
minutes with a heaped dessert-spoonful of soda. Put
the infusion into the churn with one pound of butter
and a small tablespoonful of salt. Churn until as
thick as cream.' Tea made after this fashion holds
the second place to *chang* in Tibetan affections. The
butter according to our thinking is always rancid, the
mode of making it is uncleanly, and it always has
a rank flavour from the goatskin in which it was kept.
Its value is enhanced by age. I saw skins of it forty,
fifty, and even sixty years old, which were very
highly prized, and would only be opened at some
special family festival or funeral.

During the three days of our visits to Hundar both
men and women wore their festival dresses, and apparently abandoned most of their ordinary occupations
in our honour. The men were very anxious that
I should be 'amused,' and made many grotesque
suggestions on the subject. 'Why is the European

woman always writing or sewing?' they asked. 'Is she very poor, or has she made a vow?' Visits to some of the neighbouring monasteries were eventually proposed, and turned out most interesting.

The monastery of Deskyid, to which we made a three days' expedition, is from its size and picturesque situation the most imposing in Nubra. Built on a majestic spur of rock rising on one side 2,000 feet perpendicularly from a torrent, the spur itself having an altitude of 11,000 feet, with red peaks, snow-capped, rising to a height of over 20,000 feet behind the vast irregular pile of red, white, and yellow temples, towers, storehouses, cloisters, galleries, and balconies, rising for 300 feet one above another, hanging over chasms, built out on wooden buttresses, and surmounted with flags, tridents, and *yaks'* tails, a central tower or keep dominating the whole, it is perhaps the most picturesque object I have ever seen, well worth the crossing of the Shayok fords, my painful accident, and much besides. It looks inaccessible, but in fact can be attained by rude zigzags of a thousand steps of rock, some natural, others roughly hewn, getting worse and worse as they rise higher, till the later zigzags suggest the difficulties of the ascent of the Great Pyramid. The day was fearfully hot, 99° in the shade, and the naked, shining surfaces

of purple rock with a metallic lustre radiated heat.
My 'gallant grey' took me up half-way—a great
feat—and the Tibetans cheered and shouted '*Shar-baz!*' ('Well done!') as he pluckily leapt up the
great slippery rock ledges. After I dismounted, any
number of willing hands hauled and helped me up
the remaining horrible ascent, the rugged rudeness of
which is quite indescribable. The inner entrance is
a gateway decorated with a *yak's* head and many
Buddhist emblems. High above, on a rude gallery,
fifty monks were gathered with their musical instru-
ments. As soon as the *Kan-po* or abbot, Punt-sog-sogman (the most perfect Merit), received us at the
gate, the monkish orchestra broke forth in a tornado
of sound of a most tremendous and thrilling quality,
which was all but overwhelming, as the mountain
echoes took up and prolonged the sound of fearful
blasts on six-foot silver horns, the bellowing thunder
of six-foot drums, the clash of cymbals, and the
dissonance of a number of monster gongs. It was not
music, but it was sublime. The blasts on the horns
are to welcome a great personage, and such to the
monks who despised his teaching was the devout and
learned German missionary. Mr. Redslob explained
that I had seen much of Buddhism in Ceylon and
Japan, and wished to see their temples. So with our

train of *gopas, zemindar*, peasants, and muleteers, we
mounted to a corridor full of *lamas* in ragged red

SOME INSTRUMENTS OF BUDDHIST WORSHIP

dresses, yellow girdles, and yellow caps, where we
were presented with plates of apricots, and the door

of the lowest of the seven temples heavily grated backwards.

The first view, and indeed the whole view of this temple of *Wrath* or *Justice*, was suggestive of a frightful *Inferno*, with its rows of demon gods, hideous beyond Western conception, engaged in torturing writhing and bleeding specimens of humanity. Demon masks of ancient lacquer hung from the pillars, naked swords gleamed in motionless hands, and in a deep recess whose 'darkness' was rendered 'visible' by one lamp, was that indescribable horror the executioner of the Lord of Hell, his many brandished arms holding instruments of torture, and before him the bell, the thunderbolt and sceptre, the holy water, and the baptismal flagon. Our joss-sticks fumed on the still air, monks waved censers, and blasts of dissonant music woke the semi-subterranean echoes. In this temple of Justice the younger *lamas* spend some hours daily in the supposed contemplation of the torments reserved for the unholy. In the highest temple, that of Peace, the summer sunshine fell on Shakya Thubba and the Buddhist triad seated in endless serenity. The walls were covered with frescoes of great *lamas*, and a series of alcoves, each with an image representing an incarnation of Buddha, ran round the temple. In a chapel full of monstrous images and piles of medallions made of the ashes of 'holy' men, the sub-abbot was discoursing to the acolytes on the religious classics. In the chapel of meditations, among lighted incense sticks, monks seated before images were telling their beads with the object of working themselves into a state of ecstatic contemplation (somewhat resembling a certain hypnotic trance), for there are undoubtedly devout *lamas*, though the majority are idle and unholy. It must be understood that all Tibetan literature is 'sacred,' though some of the volumes of exquisite calligraphy on parchment, which for our benefit were divested of their silken and brocaded wrappings, contain nothing better than fairy tales and stories of doubtful morality, which are recited by the *lamas* to the accompaniment of incessant cups of *chang*, as a religious duty when they visit their 'flocks' in the winter.

The Deskyid *gonpo* contains 150 *lamas*, all of whom have been educated at Lhassa. A younger son in every household becomes a monk, and occasionally enters upon his vocation as an acolyte pupil as soon as weaned. At the age of thirteen these acolytes are sent to study at Lhassa for five or seven years, their departure being made the occasion of a great village feast, with several days of religious observances. The close connection with Lhassa, especially in the case of the yellow *lamas,* gives Nubra Buddhism a singular interest. All the larger *gonpos* have their prototype in Lhassa, all ceremonial has originated in Lhassa, every instrument of worship has been consecrated in Lhassa, and every *lama* is educated in the learning only to be obtained at Lhassa. Buddhism is indeed the most salient feature of Nubra. There are *gonpos* everywhere, the roads are lined by miles of *chod-tens, manis,* and prayer-mills, and flags inscribed with sacred words in Sanskrit flutter from every roof. There are processions of red and yellow *lamas*; every act in trade, agriculture, and social life needs the sanction of sacerdotalism ; whatever exists of wealth is in the *gonpos,* which also have a monopoly of learning, and 11,000 monks closely linked with the laity, yet ruling all affairs of life and death and beyond death, are all connected by education, tradition, and authority with Lhassa.

We remained long on the blazing roof of the highest tower of the *gonpo,* while good Mr. Redslob disputed with the abbot 'concerning the things pertaining to the kingdom of God.' The monks standing round laughed sneeringly. They had shown a little interest, Mr. R. said, on his earlier visits. The abbot accepted a copy of the Gospel of St. John. ' St. Matthew,' he observed, 'is very laughable reading.' Blasts of wild music and the braying of colossal horns honoured our departure, and our difficult descent to the apricot groves of Deskyid. On our return to Hundar the grain was ripe on Gergan's fields. The first ripe ears were cut off, offered to the family divinity, and were then bound to the pillars of the house. In the comparatively fertile Nubra valley the wheat and barley are cut, not rooted up. While they cut the grain the men chant, 'May it increase, We will give to the poor, we will give to the *lamas*,' with every stroke. They believe that it can be made to multiply both under the sickle and in the threshing, and perform many religious rites for its increase while it is in sheaves. After eight days the corn is trodden out by oxen on a threshing-floor renewed every year. After winnowing with wooden forks, they make the grain into a pyramid, insert a sacred symbol, and pile upon it the threshing instruments and sacks, erecting an axe on the apex with its blade turned to the west, as that is the quarter from which demons are supposed to come. In the afternoon they feast round it, always giving a portion to the axe, saying, 'It is yours, it belongs not to me.' At dusk they pour it into the sacks again, chanting, 'May it increase.' But these are not removed to the granary until late at night, at an hour when the hands of the demons are too much

benumbed by the nightly frost to diminish the store.
At the beginning of every one of these operations
the presence of *lamas* is essential, to announce the
auspicious moment, and conduct religious ceremonies.
They receive fees, and are regaled with abundant
chang and the fat of the land.

In Hundar, as elsewhere, we were made very welcome in all the houses. I have described the dwelling
of Gergan. The poorer peasants occupy similar
houses, but roughly built, and only two-storeyed, and
the floors are merely clay. In them also the very
numerous lower rooms are used for cattle and fodder
only, while the upper part consists of an inner or
winter room, an outer or supper room, a verandah
room, and a family temple. Among their rude
plenishings are large stone corn chests like sarco-
phagi, stone bowls from Baltistan, cauldrons, cooking
pots, a tripod, wooden bowls, spoons, and dishes,
earthen pots, and *yaks'* and sheep's packsaddles. The
garments of the household are kept in long wooden
boxes.

Family life presents some curious features. In the
disposal in marriage of a girl, her eldest brother has
more 'say' than the parents. The eldest son brings
home the bride to his father's house, but at a given
age the old people are 'shelved,' i. e. they retire to

a small house, which may be termed a 'jointure house,' and the eldest son assumes the patrimony and the rule of affairs. I have not met with a similar custom anywhere in the East. It is difficult to speak of Tibetan life, with all its affection and jollity, as '*family life*,' for Buddhism, which enjoins monastic life, and usually celibacy along with it, on eleven thousand out of a total population of a hundred and twenty thousand, farther restrains the increase of population within the limits of sustenance by inculcating and rigidly upholding the system of polyandry, permitting marriage only to the eldest son, the heir of the land, while the bride accepts all his brothers as inferior or subordinate husbands, thus attaching the whole family to the soil and family roof-tree, the children being regarded legally as the property of the eldest son, who is addressed by them as 'Big Father,' his brothers receiving the title of 'Little Father.' The resolute determination, on economic as well as religious grounds, not to abandon this ancient custom, is the most formidable obstacle in the way of the reception of Christianity by the Tibetans. The women cling to it. They say, 'We have three or four men to help us instead of one,' and sneer at the dulness and monotony of European monogamous life! A woman said to me, 'If I had

MONASTIC BUILDINGS AT BASGU

only one husband, and he died, I should be a widow;
if I have two or three I am never a widow!' The
word 'widow' is with them a term of reproach, and is
applied abusively to animals and men. Children are
brought up to be very obedient to fathers and mother,
and to take great care of little ones and cattle.
Parental affection is strong. Husbands and wives
beat each other, but separation usually follows
a violent outbreak of this kind. It is the custom
for the men and women of a village to assemble
when a bride enters the house of her husbands, each
of them presenting her with three rupees. The
Tibetan wife, far from spending these gifts on personal adornment, looks ahead, contemplating possible
contingencies, and immediately hires a field, the produce of which is her own, and which accumulates
year after year in a separate granary, so that she may
not be portionless in case she leaves her husband!

It was impossible not to become attached to the
Nubra people, we lived so completely among them,
and met with such unbounded goodwill. Feasts
were given in our honour, every *gonpo* was open
to us, monkish blasts on colossal horns brayed out
welcomes, and while nothing could exceed the helpfulness and alacrity of kindness shown by all, there
was not a thought or suggestion of *backsheesh.* The

men of the villages always sat by our camp-fires at
night, friendly and jolly, but never obtrusive, telling
stories, discussing local news and the oppressions
exercised by the Kashmiri officials, the designs of
Russia, the advance of the Central Asian Railway,
and what they consider as the weakness of the Indian
Government in not annexing the provinces of the
northern frontier. Many of their ideas and feelings
are akin to ours, and a mutual understanding is
not only possible, but inevitable [1].

Industry in Nubra is the condition of existence,
and both sexes work hard enough to give a great
zest to the holidays on religious festival days.
Whether in the house or journeying the men are
never seen without the distaff. They weave also,
and make the clothes of the women and children!
The people are all cultivators, and make money
also by undertaking the transit of the goods of the
Yarkand traders over the lofty passes. The men

---

[1] Mr. Redslob said that when on different occasions he was smitten
by heavy sorrows, he felt no difference between the Tibetan feeling and
expression of sympathy and that of Europeans. A stronger testimony
to the effect produced by his twenty-five years of loving service could
scarcely be given than our welcome in Nubra. During the dangerous
illness which followed, anxious faces thronged his humble doorway as
early as break of day, and the stream of friendly inquiries never ceased
till sunset, and when he died the people of Ladak and Nubra wept and
'made a great mourning for him,' as for their truest friend.

plough with the *zho*, or hybrid *yak*, and the women break the clods and share in all other agricultural operations. The soil, destitute of manure, which is dried and hoarded for fuel, rarely produces more than tenfold. The 'three acres and a cow' is with them four acres of alluvial soil to a family on an average, with 'runs' for *yaks* and sheep on the mountains. The farms, planted with apricot and other fruit trees, a prolific loose-grained barley, wheat, peas, and lucerne, are oases in the surrounding deserts. The people export apricot oil, dried apricots, sheep's wool, heavy undyed woollens, a coarse cloth made from *yaks'* hair, and *pashm*, the under fleece of the shawl goat. They complained, and I think with good reason, of the merciless exactions of the Kashmiri officials, but there were no evidences of severe poverty, and not one beggar was seen.

It was not an easy matter to get back to Leh. The rise of the Shayok made it impossible to reach and return by the Digar Pass, and the alternative route over the Kharzong glacier continued for some time impracticable—that is, it was perfectly smooth ice. At length the news came that a fall of snow had roughened its surface. A number of men worked for two days at scaffolding a path, and with great

difficulty, and the loss of one *yak* from a falling
rock, a fruitful source of fatalities in Tibet, we
reached Khalsar, where with great regret we parted
with *Tse-ring-don-drub* (Life's purpose fulfilled), the
gopa of Sati, whose friendship had been a real
pleasure, and to whose courage and promptitude, in
Mr. Redslob's opinion, I owed my rescue from drown-
ing.   Two days of very severe marching and long
and steep ascents brought us to the wretched hamlet
of Kharzong Lar-sa, in a snowstorm, at an altitude
higher than the summit of Mont Blanc.   The servants
were all ill of 'pass-poison,' and crept into a cave along
with a number of big Tibetan mastiffs, where they
enjoyed the comfort of semi-suffocation till the next
morning, Mr. R. and I, with some willing Tibetan
helpers, pitching our own tents.   The wind was strong
and keen, and with the mercury down at 15° Fahren-
heit it was impossible to do anything but to go to bed
in the early afternoon, and stay there till the next day.
Mr. Redslob took a severe chill, which produced an
alarming attack of pleurisy, from the effects of which
he never fully recovered.

We started on a grim snowy morning, with six *yaks*
carrying our baggage or ridden by ourselves, four led
horses, and a number of Tibetans, several more having
been sent on in advance to cut steps in the glacier

and roughen them with gravel. Within certain limits the ground grows greener as one ascends, and we passed upwards among primulas, asters, a large blue myosotis, gentians, potentillas, and great sheets of *edelweiss*. At the glacier foot we skirted a deep green lake on snow with a glorious view of the Kharzong glacier and the pass, a nearly perpendicular wall of rock, bearing up a steep glacier and a snowfield of great width and depth, above which tower pinnacles of naked rock. It presented to all appearance an impassable barrier rising 2,500 feet above the lake, grand and awful in the dazzling whiteness of the new-fallen snow. Thanks to the ice steps our *yaks* took us over in four hours without a false step, and from the summit, a sharp ridge 17,500 feet in altitude, we looked our last on grimness, blackness, and snow, and southward for many a weary mile to the Indus valley lying in sunshine and summer. Fully two dozen carcases of horses newly dead lay in cavities of the glacier. Our animals were ill of ' pass-poison,' and nearly blind, and I was obliged to ride my *yak* into Leh, a severe march of thirteen hours, down miles of crumbling zigzags, and then among villages of irrigated terraces, till the grand view of the Gyalpo's palace, with its air-hung *gonpo* and clustering *chod-tens*, and of the desert city itself, burst suddenly upon

us, and our benumbed and stiffened limbs thawed in
the hot sunshine. I pitched my tent in a poplar
grove for a fortnight, near the Moravian compounds
and close to the travellers' bungalow, in which is
a British Postal Agency, with a Tibetan postmaster
who speaks English, a Christian, much trusted and
respected, named Joldan, in whose intelligence, kindness, and friendship I found both interest and pleasure.

THE YAK (*Bos grunniens*)

CHAPTER IV

JOLDAN, the Tibetan British postmaster in Leh, is
a Christian of spotless reputation. Every one places
unlimited confidence in his integrity and truthful-
ness, and his religious sincerity has been attested by
many sacrifices. He is a Ladaki, and the family
property was at Stok, a few miles from Leh. He
was baptized in Lahul at twenty-three, his father
having been a Christian. He learned Urdu, and
was for ten years mission schoolmaster in Kylang,
but returned to Leh a few years ago as postmaster.
His 'ancestral dwelling' at Stok was destroyed by
order of the wazir, and his property confiscated, after
many unsuccessful efforts had been made to win
him back to Buddhism. Afterwards he was detained
by the wazir, and compelled to serve as a sepoy,
till Mr. Heyde went to the council and obtained his

release.   His house in Leh has been more than once
burned by incendiaries.   But he pursues a quiet,
even course, brings up his family after the best
Christian traditions, refuses Buddhist suitors for

A CHANG-PA WOMAN

his daughters, unobtrusively but capably helps the
Moravian missionaries, supports his family by steady
industry, although of noble birth, and asks nothing

of any one. His 'good morning' and 'good night,' as he daily passed my tent with clockwork regularity, were full of cheery friendliness; he gave much useful information about Tibetan customs, and his ready helpfulness greatly facilitated the difficult arrangements for my farther journey.

The Leh, which I had left so dull and quiet, was full of strangers, traffic, and noise. The neat little Moravian church was filled by a motley crowd each Sunday, in which the few Christians were distinguishable by their clean faces and clothes and their devout air; and the Medical Mission Hospital and Dispensary, which in winter have an average attendance of only a hundred patients a month, were daily thronged with natives of India and Kashmir, Baltis, Yarkandis, Dards, and Tibetans. In my visits with Dr. Marx I observed, what was confirmed by four months' experience of the Tibetan villagers, that rheumatism, inflamed eyes and eyelids, and old age are the chief Tibetan maladies. Some of the Dards and Baltis were lepers, and the natives of India brought malarial fever, dysentery, and other serious diseases. The hospital, which is supported by the Indian Government, is most comfortable, a haven of rest for those who fall sick by the way. The hospital assistants are intelligent, thoroughly kind-hearted young Tibetans, who, by dint of careful drilling and an affectionate desire to please 'the teacher with the medicine box,' have become fairly trustworthy. They are not Christians.

In the neat dispensary at 9 a.m. a gong summons the patients to the operating room for a short religious service. Usually about fifty were present, and a number more, who had some curiosity about 'the way,' but did not care to be seen at Christian worship, hung about the doorways. Dr. Marx read a few verses from the Gospels, explaining them in a homely manner, and concluded with the Lord's Prayer. Then the out-patients were carefully and gently treated, leprous limbs were bathed and anointed, the wards were visited at noon and again at sunset, and in the afternoons operations were performed with the most careful antiseptic precautions, which are supposed to be used for the purpose of keeping away evil spirits from the wounds! The Tibetans, in practice, are very simple in their applications of medical remedies. Rubbing with butter is their great panacea. They have a dread of small-pox, and instead of burning its victims they throw them into their rapid torrents. If an isolated case occur, the sufferer is carried to a mountain-top, where he is left to recover or die.

If a small-pox epidemic is in the province, the people of the villages in which it has not yet appeared place thorns on their bridges and boundaries, to scare away the evil spirits which are supposed to carry the disease. In ordinary illnesses, if butter taken internally as well as rubbed into the skin does not cure the patient, the *lamas* are summoned to the rescue. They make a *mitsap*, a half life-size figure of the sick person, dress it in his or her clothes and ornaments, and place it in the courtyard, where they sit round it, reading passages from the sacred classics fitted for the occasion. After a time, all rise except the superior *lama*, who continues reading, and taking small drums in their left hands, they recite incantations, and dance wildly round the *mitsap*, believing, or at least leading the people to believe, that by this ceremony the malady, supposed to be the work of a demon, will be transferred to the image. Afterwards the clothes and ornaments are presented to them, and the figure is carried in procession out of the yard and village and is burned. If the patient becomes worse, the friends are apt to resort to the medical skill of the missionaries. If he dies they are blamed, and if he recovers the *lamas* take the credit.

At some little distance outside Leh are the cremation grounds—desert places, destitute of any other vegetation than the *Caprifolia horrida*. Each family has its furnace kept in good repair. The place is doleful, and a funeral scene on the only sunless day I experienced in Ladak was indescribably dismal. After death no one touches the corpse but the *lamas*, who assemble in numbers in the case of a rich man. The senior *lama* offers the first prayers, and lifts the lock which all Tibetans wear at the back of the head, in order to liberate the soul if it is still clinging to the body. At the same time he touches the region of the heart with a dagger. The people believe that a drop of blood on the head marks the spot where the soul has made its exit. Any good clothing in which the person has died is then removed. The blacksmith beats a drum, and the corpse, covered with a white sheet next the dress and a coloured one above, is carried out of the house to be worshipped by the relatives, who walk seven times round it. The women then retire to the house, and the chief *lama* recites liturgical passages from the formularies. Afterwards, the relatives retire, and the corpse is carried to the burning-ground by men who have the same tutelar deity as the deceased. The leading *lama* walks first, then come men with flags, followed by the blacksmith with the drum, and next the corpse, with another man beating a drum behind it. Meanwhile, the *lamas* are praying for the repose and quieting of the soul, which is hovering about, desiring to return. The attendant friends, each of whom has carried a piece of wood to the burning-ground, arrange the fuel with butter on the furnace, the corpse wrapped in the white sheet is put in, and fire is applied. The process of destruction in a rich man's case takes about an hour. During the burning the *lamas* read in high, hoarse monotones, and the blacksmiths beat their drums. The *lamas* depart first, and the blacksmiths, after worshipping the ashes, shout, ' Have nothing to do with us now,' and run rapidly away. At dawn the following day, a man whose business it is searches among the ashes for the footprints of animals, and according to the footprints found, so it is believed will be the re-birth of the soul.

Some of the ashes are taken to the *gonpos*, where the *lamas* mix them with clay, put them into oval or circular moulds, and stamp them with the image of Buddha. These are preserved in *chod-tens*, and in the house of the nearest relative of the deceased ; but in the case of 'holy' men, they are retained in

the *gonpos*, where they can be purchased by the
devout. After a cremation much *chang* is consumed
by the friends, who make presents to the bereaved
family. The value of each is carefully entered in
a book, so that a precise return may be made when
a similar occasion occurs. Until the fourth day
after death it is believed to be impossible to quiet
the soul. On that day a piece of paper is inscribed
with prayers and requests to the soul to be quiet,
and this is burned by the *lamas* with suitable
ceremonies; and rites of a more or less elaborate
kind are afterwards performed for the repose of the
soul, accompanied with prayers that it may get
'a good path' for its re-birth, and food is placed
in conspicuous places about the house, that it may
understand that its relatives are willing to support
it. The mourners for some time wear wretched
clothes, and neither dress their hair nor wash their
faces. Every year the *lamas* sell by auction the
clothing and ornaments, which are their perquisites
at funerals [1].

The Moravian missionaries have opened a school
in Leh, and the wazir, finding that the Leh people

[1] For these and other curious details concerning Tibetan customs
I am indebted to the kindness and careful investigations of the late
Rev. W. Redslob, of Leh, and the Rev. A. Heyde, of Kylang.

are the worst educated in the country, ordered that
one child at least in each family should be sent to
it. This awakened grave suspicions, and the people
hunted for reasons for it. 'The boys are to be
trained as porters, and made to carry burdens over
the mountains,' said some. 'Nay,' said others,
'they are to be sent to England and made Christians
of.' [All foreigners, no matter what their nationality
is, are supposed to be English.] Others again said,
'They are to be kidnapped,' and so the decree was
ignored, till Mr. Redslob and Dr. Marx went among
the parents and explained matters, and a large
attendance was the result; for the Tibetans of the
trade route have come to look upon the acquisition
of 'foreign learning' as the stepping-stone to Government appointments at ten rupees per month. Attendance on religious instruction was left optional, but
after a time sixty pupils were regularly present at
the daily reading and explanation of the Gospels.
Tibetan fathers teach their sons to write, to read
the sacred classics, and to calculate with a frame
of balls on wires. If farther instruction is thought
desirable, the boys are sent to the *lamas*, and even
to the schools at Lhassa. The Tibetans willingly
receive and read translations of our Christian
books, and some go so far as to think that their

teachings are 'stronger' than those of their own,
indicating their opinions by tearing pages out of
the Gospels and rolling them up into pills, which
are swallowed in the belief that they are an

CHANG-PA CHIEF

effective charm.　Sorcery is largely used in the
treatment of the sick.　The books which instruct
in the black art are known as 'black books.'

Those which treat of medicine are termed 'blue books.' Medical knowledge is handed down from father to son. The doctors know the virtues of many of the plants of the country, quantities of which they mix up together while reciting magical formulas.

I was heartily sorry to leave Leh, with its dazzling skies and abounding colour and movement, its stirring topics of talk, and the culture and exceeding kindness of the Moravian missionaries. Helpfulness was the rule. Gergan came over the Kharzong glacier on purpose to bring me a prayer-wheel; Lob-sang and Tse-ring-don-drub, the hospital assistants, made me a tent carpet of *yak's* hair cloth, singing as they sewed; and Joldan helped to secure transport for the twenty-two days' journey to Kylang. Leh has few of what Europeans regard as travelling necessaries. The brick tea which I purchased from a Lhassa trader was disgusting. I afterwards understood that blood is used in making up the blocks. The flour was gritty, and a leg of mutton turned out to be a limb of a goat of much experience. There were no straps, or leather to make them of, in the bazaar, and no buckles; and when the latter were provided by Mr. Redslob, the old man who came to sew them upon a warm rug which I had made for Gyalpo out of

pieces of carpet and hair-cloth put them on wrongly
three times, saying after each failure, 'I'm very
foolish.   Foreign ways are so wonderful!'   At times
the Tibetans say, 'We're as stupid as oxen,' and
I was inclined to think so, as I stood for two hours
instructing the blacksmith about making shoes for
Gyalpo, which kept turning out either too small for
a mule or too big for a dray-horse.

I obtained two Lahul muleteers with four horses,
quiet, obliging men, and two superb *yaks*, which were
loaded with twelve days' hay and barley for my
horse.   Provisions for the whole party for the same
time had to be carried, for the route is over an unin-
habited and arid desert.   Not the least important part
of my outfit was a letter from Mr. Redslob to the
headman or chief of the Chang-pas or Champas, the
nomadic tribes of Rupchu, to whose encampment
I purposed to make a *détour*.   These nomads had on
two occasions borrowed money from the Moravian
missionaries for the payment of the Kashmiri tribute,
and had repaid it before it was due, showing much
gratitude for the loans.

Dr. Marx accompanied me for the three first days.
The few native Christians in Leh assembled in the
gay garden plot of the lowly mission-house to shake
hands and wish me a good journey, and not a few

who were not Christians, some of them walking for the
first hour beside our horses. The road from Leh
descends to a rude wooden bridge over the Indus,
a mighty stream even there, over blazing slopes of
gravel dignified by colossal *manis* and *chod-tens* in
long lines, built by the former kings of Ladak. On
the other side of the river gravel slopes ascend
towards red mountains 20,000 feet in height. Then
comes a rocky spur crowned by the imposing castle of
the Gyalpo, the son of the dethroned king of Ladak,
surmounted by a forest of poles from which flutter
yaks' tails and long streamers inscribed with prayers.
Others bear aloft the trident, the emblem of Siva.
Carefully hewn zigzags, entered through a much-
decorated and colossal *chod-ten*, lead to the castle.
The village of Stok, the prettiest and most prosperous
in Ladak, fills up the mouth of a gorge with its large
farm-houses among poplar, apricot, and willow plantations, and irrigated terraces of barley; and is imposing
as well as pretty, for the two roads by which it is
approached are avenues of lofty *chod-tens* and broad
manis, all in excellent repair. Knolls, and deeply
coloured spurs of naked rock, most picturesquely
crowded with *chod-tens*, rise above the greenery,
breaking the purple gloom of the gorge which cuts
deeply into the mountains, and supplies from its

rushing glacier torrent the living waters which create this delightful oasis.

The *gopa* came forth to meet us, bearing apricots and cheeses as the Gyalpo's greeting, and conducted us to the camping-ground, a sloping lawn in a willow-wood, with many a natural bower of the graceful *Clematis orientalis.* The tents were pitched, after-noon tea was on a table outside, a clear, swift stream made fitting music, the dissonance of the ceaseless beating of gongs and drums in the castle temple was softened by distance, the air was cool, a lemon light bathed the foreground, and to the north, across the Indus, the great mountains of the Leh range, with every cleft defined in purple or blue, lifted their vermilion peaks into a rosy sky. It was the poetry and luxury of travel.

At Leh I was obliged to dismiss the *seis* for pro-longed misconduct and cruelty to Gyalpo, and Mando undertook to take care of him. The animal had always been held by two men while the *seis* groomed him with difficulty, but at Stok, when Mando rubbed him down, he quietly went on feeding and laid his lovely head on the lad's shoulder with a soft cooing sound. From that moment Mando could do anything with him, and a singular attachment grew up between man and horse.

Towards sunset we were received by the Gyalpo. The castle loses nothing of its picturesqueness on a nearer view, and everything about it is trim and in good order. It is a substantial mass of stone building on a lofty rock, the irregularities of which have been taken most artistic advantage of in order to give picturesque irregularity to the edifice, which, while six storeys high in some places, is only three in others. As in the palace of Leh, the walls slope inwards from the base, where they are ten feet thick, and projecting balconies of brown wood and grey stone relieve their monotony. We were received at the entrance by a number of red *lamas*, who took us up five flights of rude stairs to the reception room, where we were introduced to the Gyalpo, who was in the midst of a crowd of monks, and, except that his hair was not shorn, and that he wore a silver brocade cap and large gold earrings and bracelets, was dressed in red like them. Throneless and childless, the Gyalpo has given himself up to religion. He has covered the castle roof with Buddhist emblems (not represented in the sketch). From a pole, forty feet long, on the terrace floats a broad streamer of equal length, completely covered with *Aum mani padne hun*, and he has surrounded himself with *lamas*, who conduct nearly ceaseless services in the sanctuary. The

attainment of merit, as his creed leads him to understand it, is his one aim in life.   He loves the seclusion
of Stok, and rarely visits the palace in Leh, except at
the time of the winter games, when the whole population assembles in cheery, orderly crowds, to witness
races, polo and archery matches, and a species of
hockey.   He interests himself in the prosperity of
Stok, plants poplars, willows, and fruit trees, and
keeps the castle *manis* and *chod-tens* in admirable
repair.

Stok Castle is as massive as any of our mediaeval
buildings, but is far lighter and roomier.   It is most
interesting to see a style of architecture and civilisation which bears not a solitary trace of European
influence, not even in Manchester cottons or Russian
gimcracks.   The Gyalpo's room was only roofed for
six feet within the walls, where it was supported by
red pillars.   Above, the deep blue Tibetan sky was
flushing with the red of sunset, and from a noble
window with a covered stone balcony there was an
enchanting prospect of red ranges passing into trans-
lucent amethyst.   The partial ceiling is painted in
arabesques, and at one end of the room is an alcove,
much enriched with bold wood carving.

The Gyalpo was seated on a carpet on the floor,
a smooth-faced, rather stupid-looking man of twenty-

THE CASTLE OF STOK

eight. He placed us on a carpet beside him, and coffee, honey, and apricots were brought in, but the conversation flagged. He neither suggested anything nor took up Dr. Marx's suggestions. Fortunately, we had brought our sketch-books, and the views of several places were recognised, and were found interesting. The *lamas* and servants, who had remained respectfully standing, sat down on the floor, and even the Gyalpo became animated. So our visit ended successfully.

There is a doorway from the reception room into the sanctuary, and after a time fully thirty *lamas* passed in and began service, but the Gyalpo only stood on his carpet. There is only a half light in this temple, which is further obscured by scores of smoked and dusty bannerets of gold and silver brocade hanging from the roof. In addition to the usual Buddhist emblems there are musical instruments, exquisitely inlaid, or enriched with *niello* work of gold and silver of great antiquity, and bows of singular strength, requiring two men to bend them, which are made of small pieces of horn cleverly joined. *Lamas* gabbled liturgies at railroad speed, beating drums and clashing cymbals as an accompaniment, while others blew occasional blasts on the colossal silver horns or trumpets, which probably resemble those with which Jericho was encompassed. The music, the discordant and high-pitched monotones, and the revolting odours of stale smoke of juniper chips, of rancid butter, and of unwashed woollen clothes which drifted through the doorway, were overpowering. Attempted fights among the horses woke me often during the night, and the sound of worship was always borne over the still air.

Dr. Marx left on the third day, after we had visited the monastery of Hemis, the richest in Ladak, holding large landed property and possessing much metallic wealth, including a *chod-ten* of silver and gold, thirty feet high, in one of its many halls, approached by gold-plated silver steps and incrusted with precious stones; there is also much fine work in brass and bronze. Hemis abounds in decorated buildings most picturesquely placed, it has three hundred *lamas*, and is regarded as 'the sight' of Ladak.

At Upschi, after a day's march over blazing gravel, I left the rushing olive-green Indus, which I had followed from the bridge of Khalsi, where a turbulent torrent, the Upshi water, joins it, descending through a gorge so narrow that the track, which at all times is blasted on the face of the precipice, is occasionally scaffolded. A very extensive rock-slip had carried away the path and rendered several fords necessary, and before I reached it rumour was busy with the peril. It was true that the day before several mules had been carried away and drowned, that many loads had been sacrificed, and that one native traveller had lost his life. So I started my caravan at daybreak, to get the water at its lowest, and ascended the gorge, which is an absolutely verdureless rift in mountains of most brilliant and fantastic stratification. At the first ford Mando was carried down the river for a short distance. The second was deep and strong, and a caravan of valuable goods had been there for two days, afraid to risk the crossing. My Lahulis, who always showed a great lack of stamina, sat down, sobbing and beating their breasts. Their sole wealth, they said, was in their baggage animals, and the river was 'wicked,' and 'a demon' lived in it who paralysed the horses' legs. Much experience of Orientals and of travel has taught me to surmount difficulties in my own way, so, beckoning to two men from the opposite side, who came over shakily with linked arms, I took the two strong ropes which I always carry on my saddle, and roped these men together and to Gyalpo's halter with one, and lashed Mando and the guide together with the other, giving them the stout thongs behind the saddle to hold on to, and in this compact mass we stood the strong rush of the river safely, the paralysing chill of its icy waters being a far more obvious peril. All the baggage animals were brought over in the same way, and the Lahulis praised their gods.

At Gya, a wild hamlet, the last in Ladak proper, I met a working naturalist whom I had seen twice before, and 'forgathered' with him much of the way. Eleven days of solitary desert succeeded. The reader has probably understood that no part of the Indus, Shayok, and Nubra valleys, which make up most of the province of Ladak, is less than 9,500 feet in altitude, and that the remainder is composed of precipitous mountains with glaciers and snowfields, ranging from 18,000 to 25,000 feet, and that the villages are built mainly on alluvial soil where possibilities of irrigation exist. But Rupchu has peculiarities of its own.

Between Gya and Darcha, the first hamlet in Lahul, are three huge passes, the Toglang, 18,150 feet in altitude, the Lachalang, 17,500, and the Baralacha, 16,000,—all easy, except for the difficulties arising from the highly rarefied air. The mountains of the region, which are from 20,000 to 23,000 feet in altitude, are seldom precipitous or picturesque, except the huge red needles which guard the Lachalang Pass, but are rather 'monstrous protuberances,' with arid

surfaces of disintegrated rock. Among these are
remarkable plateaux, which are taken advantage of
by caravans, and which have elevations of from 14,000
to 15,000 feet. There are few permanent rivers or
streams, the lakes are salt, beside the springs, and
on the plateaux there is scanty vegetation, chiefly
aromatic herbs ; but on the whole Rupchu is a desert
of arid gravel. Its only inhabitants are 500 nomads,
and on the ten marches of the trade route, the bridle
paths, on which in some places labour has been spent,
the tracks, not always very legible, made by the
passage of caravans, and rude dykes, behind which
travellers may shelter themselves from the wind, are
the only traces of man. Herds of the *kyang*, the
wild horse of some naturalists, and the wild ass of
others, graceful and beautiful creatures, graze within
gunshot of the track without alarm.

I had thought Ladak windy, but Rupchu is the
home of the winds, and the marches must be arranged
for the quietest time of the day. Happily the gales
blow with clockwork regularity, the day wind from
the south and south-west rising punctually at 9 a.m.
and attaining its maximum at 2.30, while the night
wind from the north and north-east rises about 9 p.m.
and ceases about 5 a.m. Perfect silence is rare. The
highly rarefied air, rushing at great speed, when at

its worst deprives the traveller of breath, skins his
face and hands, and paralyses the baggage animals.
In fact, neither man nor beast can face it. The horses
'turn tail' and crowd together, and the men build up
the baggage into a wall and crouch in the lee of it.
The heat of the solar rays is at the same time fearful.
At Lachalang, at a height of over 15,000 feet, I noted
a solar temperature of 152°, only 35° below the boiling
point of water in the same region, which is about
187°. To make up for this, the mercury falls below
the freezing point every night of the year, even in
August the difference of temperature in twelve hours
often exceeding 120° ! The Rupchu nomads, however, delight in this climate of extremes, and regard
Leh as a place only to be visited in winter, and Kulu
and Kashmir as if they were the malarial swamps of
the Congo !

We crossed the Toglang Pass, at a height of 18,150
feet, with less suffering from *ladug* than on either the
Digar or Kharzong Passes. Indeed Gyalpo carried
me over it, stopping to take breath every few yards.
It was then a long dreary march to the camping-
ground of Tsala, where the Chang-pas spend the four
summer months ; the guides and baggage animals
lost the way and did not appear until the next day,
and in consequence the servants slept unsheltered in

FIRST VILLAGE IN KULU

the snow. News travels as if by magic in desert places. Towards evening, while riding by a stream up a long and tedious valley, I saw a number of moving specks on the crest of a hill, and down came a surge of horsemen riding furiously. Just as they threatened to sweep Gyalpo away, they threw their horses on their haunches, in one moment were on the ground, which they touched with their foreheads, presented me with a plate of apricots, and the next vaulted into their saddles, and dashing up the valley were soon out of sight. In another half-hour there was a second wild rush of horsemen, the headman dismounted, threw himself on his face, kissed my hand, vaulted into the saddle, and then led a swirl of his tribesmen at a gallop in ever-narrowing circles round me till they subsided into the decorum of an escort. An elevated plateau with some vegetation on it, a row of forty tents, 'black' but not 'comely,' a bright rapid river, wild hills, long lines of white sheep converging towards the camp, *yaks* rampaging down the hillsides, men running to meet us, and women and children in the distance were singularly idealised in the golden glow of a cool, moist evening.

Two men took my bridle, and two more proceeded to put their hands on my stirrups; but Gyalpo kicked them to the right and left amidst shrieks of laughter,

after which, with frantic gesticulations and yells of
'*Kabardar!*' I was led through the river in triumph
and hauled off my horse. The tribesmen were much
excited. Some dashed about, performing feats of
horsemanship; others brought apricots and dough-
balls made with apricot oil, or rushed to the tents,
returning with rugs; some cleared the camping-
ground of stones and raised a stone platform, and
a flock of goats, exquisitely white from the daily
swims across the river, were brought to be milked.
Gradually and shrinkingly the women and children
drew near; but Mr. ——'s Bengali servant threatened
them with a whip, when there was a general stampede,
the women running like hares. I had trained my
servants to treat the natives courteously, and addressed
some rather strong language to the offender, and
afterwards succeeded in enticing all the fugitives
back by showing my sketches, which gave boundless
pleasure and led to very numerous requests for
portraits! The *gopa*, though he had the oblique
Mongolian eyes, was a handsome young man, with
a good nose and mouth. He was dressed like the
others in a girdled *chaga* of coarse serge, but wore
a red cap turned up over the ears with fine fur,
a silver inkhorn, and a Yarkand knife in a chased
silver sheath in his girdle, and canary-coloured leather

shoes with turned-up points. The people prepared
one of their own tents for me, and laying down
a number of rugs of their own dyeing and weaving,
assured me of an unbounded welcome as a friend of
their 'benefactor,' Mr. Redslob, and then proposed
that I should visit their tents accompanied by all the
elders of the tribe.

CHAPTER V

THE last chapter left me with the chief and elders of the Chang-pas starting on 'a round of visits,' and it was not till nightfall that the solemn ceremony was concluded. Each of the fifty tents was visited : at every one a huge, savage Tibetan mastiff made an attempt to fly at me, and was pounced upon and held down by a woman little bigger than himself, and in each cheese and milk were offered and refused. In all I received a hearty welcome for the sake of the 'great father,' Mr. Redslob, who designated these people as 'the simplest and kindliest people on earth.'

This Chang-pa tribe, numbering five hundred souls, makes four moves in the year, dividing in summer, and uniting in a valley very free from snow in the winter. They are an exclusively pastoral people, and possess large herds of *yaks* and ponies and immense flocks of sheep and goats, the latter almost entirely the beautiful 'shawl goat,' from the undergrowth at the base of the long hair of which the fine Kashmir shawls are made. This *pashm* is a provision which Nature makes against the intense cold of these altitudes, and grows on *yaks*, sheep, and dogs, as well as on most of the wild animals. The sheep is the big, hornless, flop-eared *huniya*. The *yaks* and sheep are the load carriers of Rupchu. Small or easily divided merchandise is carried by sheep, and bulkier goods by *yaks*, and the Chang-pas make a great deal of money by carrying for the Lahul, Central Ladak, and Rudok merchants, their sheep travelling as far as Gar in Chinese Tibet. They are paid in grain as well as coin, their own country producing no farinaceous food. They have only two uses for silver money. With part of their gains they pay the tribute to Kashmir, and they melt the rest, and work it into rude personal ornaments. According to an old arrangement between Lhassa and Leh, they carry brick tea free for the Lhassa merchants. They are Buddhists, and practise polyandry, but their young men do not become *lamas*, and owing to the scarcity of fuel, instead of burning their dead, they expose them with religious rites face upwards in desolate places, to be made away with by the birds of the air. All their tents have a god-shelf, on which are placed small images and sacred emblems. They dress as the Ladakis, except that the men wear shoes with very high turned-up points, and that the women, in addition to the *perak*, the usual ornament, place on the top of the head a large silver coronet with three tassels. In physiognomy they resemble the Ladakis, but the Mongolian type is purer, the eyes are more oblique, and the eyelids have a greater droop, the chins project more, and the mouths are handsomer. Many of the men, including the headman, were quite good-looking, but the upper lips of the women were apt to be 'tucked up,' displaying very square teeth, as we have shown in the preceding chapter.

The roofs of the Tsala tents are nearly flat, and the middle has an opening six inches wide along its whole length. An excavation from twelve to twenty-four inches deep is made in the soil, and a rude wall of stones, about one foot high, is built round it, over which the tent cloth, made in narrow widths of *yak's* or goat's hair, is extended by ropes led over forked sticks. There is no ridge pole, and the centre is supported on short poles, to the projecting tops of which prayer flags and *yaks'* tails are attached. The interior, though dark, is not too dark for weaving, and each tent has its loom, for the Chang-pas not only weave their coarse woollen clothing and hair

A TIBETAN FARM-HOUSE

cloth for saddlebags and tents, but rugs of wool dyed in rich colours made from native roots. The largest tent was twenty feet by fifteen, but the majority measured only fourteen feet by eight and ten feet. The height in no case exceeded six feet. In these much ventilated and scarcely warmed shelters these hardy nomads brave the tremendous winds and winter rigours of their climate at altitudes varying from 13,000 to 14,500 feet. Water freezes every night of the year, and continually there are differences in temperature of 100° between noon and midnight. In addition to the fifty dwelling tents there was one considerably larger, in which the people store their wool and goat's hair till the time arrives for taking them to market. The floor of several of the tents was covered with rugs, and besides looms and confused heaps of what looked like rubbish, there were tea-churns, goatskin churns, sheep and goat skins, children's bows and arrows, cooking pots, and heaps of the furze root, which is used as fuel.

They expended much of this scarce commodity upon me in their hospitality, and kept up a bonfire all night. They mounted their wiry ponies and performed feats of horsemanship, in one of which all the animals threw themselves on their hind

legs in a circle when a man in the centre clapped
his hands; and they crowded my tent to see my
sketches, and were not satisfied till I executed some
daubs professing to represent some of the elders.
The excitement of their first visit from a European
woman lasted late into the night, and when they
at last retired they persisted in placing a guard of
honour round my tent.

In the morning there was ice on the pools, and
the snow lay three inches deep. Savage life had
returned to its usual monotony, and the care of
flocks and herds. In the early afternoon the chief
and many of the men accompanied us across the
ford, and we parted with mutual expressions of good
will. The march was through broad gravelly valleys,
among 'monstrous protuberances' of red and yellow
gravel, elevated by their height alone to the dignity
of mountains. Hail came on, and Gyalpo showed
his high breeding by facing it when the other animals
'turned tail' and huddled together, and a storm of
heavy sleet of some hours' duration burst upon us
just as we reached the dismal camping-ground of Ruk-
chen, guarded by mountain giants which now and then
showed glimpses of their white skirts through the
dark driving mists. That was the only 'weather' in
four months.

A large caravan from the heat and sunshine of Amritsar was there. The goods were stacked under goat's hair shelters, the mules were huddled together without food, and their shivering Panjābi drivers, muffled in blankets which only left one eye exposed, were grubbing up furze roots wherewith to make smoky fires. My baggage, which had arrived previously, was lying soaking in the sleet, while the wretched servants were trying to pitch the tent in the high wind. They had slept out in the snow the night before, and were mentally as well as physically benumbed. Their misery had a comic side to it, and as the temperature made me feel specially well, I enjoyed bestirring myself, and terrified Mando, who was feebly 'fadding' with a rag, by giving Gyalpo a vigorous rub-down with a bath-towel. Hassan Khan, with chattering teeth and severe neuralgia, muffled in my 'fisherman's hood' under his turban, was trying to do his work with his unfailing pluck. Mando was shedding futile tears over wet furze which would not light, the small wet corrie was dotted over with the Amritsar men sheltering under rocks and nursing hopeless fires, and fifty mules and horses, with dejected heads and dripping tails, and their backs to the merciless wind, were attempting to pick some food from scanty

herbage already nibbled to the root. My tent was
a picture of grotesque discomfort. The big stones
had not been picked out from the gravel, the bed
stood in puddles, the thick horse blanket was draining
over the one chair, the servant's spare clothing and
stores were on the table, the *yaks'* loads of wet hay
and the soaked grain sack filled up most of the
space; a wet candle sputtered and went out, wet
clothes dripped from the tent hook, and every now
and then Hassan Khan looked in with one eye,
gasping out, 'Mem Sahib, I can no light the fire!'
Perseverance succeeds eventually, and cups of a strong
stimulant made of Burroughes and Wellcome's vigorous
'valoid' tincture of ginger and hot water, revived
the men all round. Such was its good but innocent
effect, that early the next morning Hassan came into
my tent with two eyes, and convulsed with laughter.
'The pony men' and Mando, he said, were crying,
and the coolie from Leh, who before the storm had
wanted to go the whole way to Simla, after refusing
his supper had sobbed all night under the 'flys' of
my tent, while I was sleeping soundly. Afterwards
I harangued them, and told them I would let them
go, and help them back; I could not take such poor-
spirited miserable creatures with me, and I would
keep the Tartars who had accompanied me from Tsala.

On this they protested, and said, with a significant gesture, I might cut their throats if they cried any more, and begged me to try them again; and as we had no more bad weather, there was no more trouble.

The marches which followed were along valleys, plains, and mountain-sides of gravel, destitute of herbage, except a shrivelled artemisia, and on one occasion the baggage animals were forty hours without food. Fresh water was usually very scarce, and on the Lingti plains was only obtainable by scooping it up from the holes left by the feet of animals. Insect life was rare, and except grey doves, the 'dove of the valleys,' which often flew before us for miles down the ravines, no birds were to be seen. On the other hand, there were numerous herds of *kyang*, which in the early mornings came to drink of the water by which the camps were pitched. By looking through a crevice of my tent I saw them distinctly, without alarming them. In one herd I counted forty. They kept together in families, sire, dam, and foal. The animal certainly is under fourteen hands, and resembles a mule rather than a horse or ass. The noise, which I had several opportunities of hearing, is more like a neigh than a bray, but lacks completeness. The creature is light brown, almost fawn colour, fading into white under his body, and he has a dark

stripe on his back, but not a cross. His ears are
long, and his tail is like that of a mule. He trots
and gallops, and when alarmed gallops fast, but as
he is not worth hunting, he has not a great dread of
humanity, and families of *kyang* frequently grazed
within two hundred and fifty yards of us. He is
about as untamable as the zebra, and with his family
affectionateness leads apparently a very happy life.

On the Kwangchu plateau, at an elevation of
15,000 feet, I met with a form of life which has
a great interest of its own, sheep caravans, numbering
among them 7,000 sheep, each animal with its wool
on, and equipped with a neat packsaddle and two
leather or hair-cloth bags, and loaded with from
twenty-five to thirty-two pounds of salt or borax.
These, and many more which we passed, were carrying
their loads to Patseo, a mountain valley in Lahul,
where they are met by traders from Northern British
India. The sheep are shorn, and the wool and loads
are exchanged for wheat and a few other commodities,
with which they return to Tibet, the whole journey
taking from nine months to a year. As the sheep
live by grazing the scanty herbage on the march,
they never accomplish more than ten miles a day,
and as they often become footsore, halts of several
days are frequently required. Sheep, dead or dying,

LAHUL VALLEY

with the birds of prey picking out their eyes, were often met with. Ordinarily these caravans are led by a man, followed by a large goat much bedecked and wearing a large bell. Each driver has charge of one hundred sheep. These men, of small stature but very thickset, with their wide smooth faces, loose clothing of sheepskin with the wool outside, with their long coarse hair flying in the wind, and their uncouth shouts in a barbarous tongue, are much like savages. They sing wild chants as they picket their sheep in long double lines at night, and with their savage mastiffs sleep unsheltered under the frosty skies under the lee of their piled-up saddlebags. On three nights I camped beside their caravans, and walked round their orderly lines of sheep and their neat walls of saddlebags ; and, far from showing any discourtesy or rude curiosity, they held down their fierce dogs and exhibited their ingenious mode of tethering their animals, and not one of the many articles which my servants were in the habit of leaving outside the tents was on any occasion abstracted. The dogs, however, were less honest than their masters, and on one night ran away with half a sheep, and I should have fared poorly had not Mr. —— shot some grey doves.

Marches across sandy and gravelly valleys, and along arid mountain-sides spotted with a creeping furze and cushions of a yellow-green moss which seems able to exist without moisture, fords of the Sumgyal and Tserap rivers, and the crossing of the Lachalang Pass at an altitude of 17,500 feet in severe frost, occupied several uneventful days. Of the three lofty passes on this route, the Toglang, which is higher, and the Baralacha, which is lower, are featureless billows of gravel, over which a carriage might easily be driven. Not so is the Lachalang, though its well-made zigzags are easy for laden animals. The approach to it is fantastic, among precipitous mountains of red sandstone, and red rocks weathered into pillars, men's heads, and numerous groups of gossipy old women from thirty to fifty feet high, in flat hats and long circular cloaks! Entering by red gates of rock into a region of gigantic mountains, and following up a crystal torrent, the valley narrowing to a gorge, and the gorge to a chasm guarded by nearly perpendicular needles of rock flaming in the westering sun, we forded the river at the chasm's throat, and camped on a velvety green lawn just large enough for a few tents, absolutely walled in by abrupt mountains 18,000 and 19,000 feet in height. Long after the twilight settled down on us, the pinnacles above glowed in warm sunshine, and the following morning, when it was only dawn below, and the still river pools were frozen and the grass was white with hoar-frost, the morning sun reddened the snow-peaks and kindled into vermilion the red needles of Lachalang. That camping-ground under such conditions is the grandest and most romantic spot of the whole journey.

Verdureless and waterless stretches, in crossing which our poor animals were two nights without food, brought us to the glacier-blue waters of the Serchu, tumbling along in a deep broad gash, and farther on to a lateral torrent which is the boundary between Rupchu, tributary to Kashmir, and Lahul or British Tibet, under the rule of the Empress of India. The tents were ready pitched in a grassy hollow by the river; horses, cows, and goats were grazing near them, and a number of men were preparing food. A Tibetan approached me, accompanied by a creature in a nondescript dress speaking Hindustani volubly. On a band across his breast were the British crown, and a plate with the words ' Commissioner's *chaprassie*, Kulu district.' I never felt so extinguished. Liberty seemed lost, and the romance of the desert to have died out in one moment! At the camping-ground I found rows of salaaming Lahulis drawn up, and Hassan Khan in a state which was a compound of pomposity and jubilant excitement. The *tahsildar* (really the Tibetan honorary magistrate), he said, had received instructions from the Lieutenant-Governor of the Panjāb that I was on the way to Kylang, and was to 'want for nothing.' So twenty-four men, nine horses, a flock of goats, and two cows had been waiting for me for three days in the Serchu valley. I wrote a polite note to the magistrate, and sent all back except the *chaprassie*, the cows, and the cow-herd, my servants looking much crestfallen.

We crossed the Baralacha Pass in wind and snow showers into a climate in which moisture began to be obvious. At short distances along the pass, which extends for many miles, there are rude semicircular walls, three feet high, all turned in one direction, in the shelter of which travellers crouch to escape from the strong cutting wind. My men suffered far more than on the two higher passes, and it was difficult to dislodge them from these shelters, where they lay groaning, gasping, and suffering from vertigo and nose-bleeding. The cold was so severe that I walked over the loftiest part of the pass, and for the first time felt slight effects of the *ladug*. At a height of 15,000 feet, in the midst of general desolation, grew, in the shelter of rocks, poppies (*Mecanopsis aculeata*), blue as the Tibetan skies, their centres filled with a cluster of golden-yellow stamens,—a most charming sight. Ten or twelve of these exquisite blossoms grow on one stalk, and stalk, leaf, and seed-vessels are guarded by very stiff thorns. Lower down flowers abounded, and at the camping-ground of Patseo (12,000 feet), where the Tibetan sheep caravans exchange their wool, salt, and borax for grain, the ground was covered with soft greensward, and real rain fell. Seen from the Baralacha Pass are vast snow-fields, glaciers, and avalanche slopes. This barrier, and the Rotang, farther south, close this trade route practically for seven months of the year, for they catch the monsoon rains, which at that altitude are snows from fifteen to thirty feet deep; while on the other side of the Baralacha and throughout Rupchu and Ladak the snowfall is insignificant. So late as August, when I crossed, there were four perfect snow bridges over the Bhaga, and snowfields thirty-six feet deep along its margin. At Patseo the *tahsildar*, with a retinue and animals laden with fodder, came to pay his respects to me, and invited me to his house, three days' journey. These were the first human beings we had seen for three days.

A few miles south of the Baralacha Pass some birch trees appeared on a slope, the first natural growth of timber that I had seen since crossing the Zoji La. Lower down there were a few more, then

stunted specimens of the pencil cedar, and the mountains began to show a shade of green on their lower
slopes. Butterflies appeared also, and a vulture, a
grand bird on the wing, hovered ominously over us
for some miles, and was succeeded by an equally
ominous raven. On the excellent bridle-track cut
on the face of the precipices which overhang the
Bhaga, there is in nine miles only one spot in which
it is possible to pitch a five-foot tent, and at Darcha,
the first hamlet in Lahul, the only camping-ground
is on the house roofs. There the Chang-pas and
their *yaks* and horses who had served me pleasantly
and faithfully from Tsala left me, and returned to
the freedom of their desert life. At Kolang, the next
hamlet, where the thunder of the Bhaga was almost
intolerable, Hara Chang, the magistrate, one of the
thakurs or feudal proprietors of Lahul, with his son
and nephew and a large retinue, called on me ; and
the next morning Mr. —— and I went by invitation
to visit him in his castle, a magnificently situated
building on a rocky spur 1,000 feet above the camping-
ground, attained by a difficult climb, and nearly on a
level with the glittering glaciers and ice-falls on the
other side of the Bhaga. It only differs from Leh
and Stok castles in having blue glass in some of the
smaller windows. In the family temple, in addition

GONPO AT KYLANG

to the usual life-size images of Buddha and the Triad, there was a female divinity, carved at Jallandhur in India, copied from a statue representing Queen Victoria in her younger days—a very fitting possession for the highest government official in Lahul. The *thakur*, Hara Chang, is wealthy and a rigid Buddhist, and uses his very considerable influence against the work of the Moravian missionaries in the valley. The rude path down to the bridle-road, through fields of barley and buckwheat, is bordered by roses, gooseberries, and masses of wild flowers.

The later marches after reaching Darcha are grand beyond all description. The track, scaffolded or blasted out of the rock at a height of from 1,000 to 3,000 feet above the thundering Bhaga, is scarcely a rifle-shot from the mountain mass dividing it from the Chandra, a mass covered with nearly unbroken ice and snowfields, out of which rise pinnacles of naked rock 21,000 and 22,000 feet in altitude. The region is the 'abode of snow,' and glaciers of great size fill up every depression. Humidity, vegetation, and beauty reappear together, wild flowers and ferns abound, and pencil cedars in clumps rise above the artificial plantations of the valley. Wheat ripens at an altitude of 12,000 feet. Picturesque villages, surrounded by orchards, adorn the mountain spurs;

chod-tens and *gonpos*, with white walls and flutter-
ing flags, brighten the scene ; feudal castles crown
the heights, and where the mountains are loftiest,
the snowfields and glaciers most imposing, and the
greenery densest, the village of Kylang, the most
important in Lahul as the centre of trade, government, and Christian missions, hangs on ledges of the
mountain-side 1,000 feet above Bhaga, whose furious
course can be traced far down the valley by flashes
of sunlit foam.

The Lahul valley, which is a part of British Tibet,
has an altitude of 10,000 feet. It prospers under
British rule, its population has increased, Hindu
merchants have settled in Kylang, the route through
Lahul to Central Asia is finding increasing favour
with the Panjābi traders, and the Moravian missionaries, by a bolder system of irrigation and the provision of storage for water, have largely increased
the quantity of arable land. The Lahulis are chiefly
Tibetans, but Hinduism is largely mixed up with
Buddhism in the lower villages. All the *gonpos*,
however, have been restored and enlarged during
the last twenty years. In winter the snow lies
fifteen feet deep, and for four or five months, owing
to the perils of the Rotang Pass, the valley rarely
has any communication with the outer world.

At the foot of the village of Kylang, which is built in tier above tier of houses up the steep side of a mountain with a height of 21,000 feet, are the Moravian mission buildings, long, low, whitewashed erections, of the simplest possible construction, the design and much of the actual erection being the work of these capable Germans. The large building, which has a deep verandah, the only place in which exercise can be taken in the winter, contains the native church, three rooms for each missionary, and two guest-rooms. Round the garden are the printing rooms, the medicine and store room (stores arriving once in two years), and another guest-room. Round an adjacent enclosure are the houses occupied in winter by the Christians when they come down with their sheep and cattle from the hill farms. All is absolutely plain, and as absolutely clean and trim. The guest-rooms and one or two of the Tibetan rooms are papered with engravings from the *Illustrated London News*, but the rooms of the missionaries are only whitewashed, and by their extreme bareness reminded me of those of very poor pastors in the Fatherland. A garden, brilliant with zinnias, dianthus, and petunias, all of immense size, and planted with European trees, is an oasis, and in it I camped for some weeks under a willow tree, covered, as many are, with a sweet secretion so abundant as to drop on the roof of the tent, and which the people collect and use as honey.

The mission party consisted of Mr. and Mrs. Shreve, lately arrived, and now in a distant exile at Poo, and Mr. and Mrs. Heyde, who had been in Tibet for nearly forty years, chiefly spent at Kylang, without going home. 'Plain living and high thinking' were the rule. Books and periodicals were numerous, and were read and assimilated. The culture was simply wonderful, and the acquaintance with the latest ideas in theology and natural science, the latest political and social developments, and the latest conceptions in European art, would have led me to suppose that these admirable people had only just left Europe. Mrs. Heyde had no servant, and in the long winters, when household and mission work are over for the day, and there are no mails to write for, she pursues her tailoring and other needlework, while her husband reads aloud till midnight. At the time of my visit (September) busy preparations for the winter were being made. Every day the wood piles grew. Hay, cut with sickles on the steep hillsides, was carried on human backs into the farmyard, apples were cored and dried in the sun, cucumbers were pickled, vinegar was made, potatoes were stored, and meat was killed and salted.

It is in winter, when the Christians have come down from the mountain, that most of the mission work is done. Mrs. Heyde has a school of forty girls, mostly Buddhists. The teaching is simple and practical, and includes the knitting of socks, of which from four to five hundred pairs are turned out each winter, and find a ready sale. The converts meet for instruction and discussion twice daily, and there is daily worship. The mission press is kept actively employed in printing the parts of the Bible which have been translated during the summer, as well as simple tracts written or translated by Mr. Heyde. No converts are better instructed, and like those of Leh they seem of good quality, and are industrious and self-supporting. Winter work is severe, as ponies, cattle, and sheep must always be hand-fed, and often hand-watered. Mr. Heyde has great repute as a doctor, and in summer people travel long distances for his advice and medicine. He is universally respected, and his judgment in worldly affairs is highly thought of; but if one were to judge merely by apparent results, the devoted labour of nearly forty years and complete self-sacrifice for the good of Kylang must be pronounced unsuccessful. Christianity has been most strongly opposed by men of influence, and converts have been exposed to persecution and loss. The abbot of the Kylang monastery lately said to Mr. Heyde, 'Your Christian teaching has given Buddhism a resurrection.' The actual words used were, 'When you came here people were quite indifferent about their religion, but since it has been attacked they have become zealous, and now they *know*.' It is only by sharing their circumstances of isolation, and by getting glimpses of their everyday life and work, that one can realise at all what the heroic perseverance and self-sacrificing toil of these forty years have been, and what is the weighty influence on the people and on the standard of morals, even though the number of converts is so small. All honour to these noble German missionaries, learned, genial, cultured, radiant, who, whether teaching, preaching, farming, gardening, printing, or doctoring, are always and everywhere 'living epistles of Christ, known and read of all men!' Close by the mission house, in a green spot under shady trees, is God's Acre, where many children of the mission families sleep, and a few adults.

As the winter is the busiest season in mission work, so it is the great time in which the *lamas* make house-to-house peregrinations and attend at festivals. Then also there is much spinning and weaving by both sexes, and tobogganing and other games, and much drinking of *chang* by priests and people. The cattle remain out till nearly Christmas, and are then taken into the houses. At the time of the variable new year, the *lamas* and nuns retire to the monasteries, and dulness reigns in the valleys. At the end of a month they emerge, life and noise begin, and all men to whom sons have been born during the previous year give *chang* freely. During the festival which follows, all these jubilant fathers go out of the village as a gaudily dressed procession, and form a circle round a picture of a *yak*, painted by the *lamas*, which is used as a target to be shot at with bows and arrows, and it is believed that the man who hits it in the centre will be blessed with a son in the coming year. After this, all the Kylang men and women collect in one house by annual rotation, and sing and drink immense quantities of *chang* till 10 p.m.

The religious festivals begin soon after. One, the worshipping of the *lamas* by the laity, occurs in every village, and lasts from two to three days. It consists chiefly of music and dancing, while the *lamas* sit in rows, swilling *chang* and arrack. At another, which is celebrated annually in every house, the *lamas* assemble, and in front of certain gods prepare a number of mystical figures made of dough,

which are hung up and are worshipped by the family.
Afterwards the *lamas* make little balls which are
worshipped, and one of the family mounts the roof
and invites the neighbours, who receive the balls
from the *lamas'* hands and drink moderately of *chang*.
Next, the figures are thrown to the demons as a
propitiatory offering, amidst 'hellish whistlings' and
the firing of guns. These ceremonies are called *ise
drup* (a full life), and it is believed that if they were
neglected life would be cut short.

One of the most important of the winter religious
duties of the *lamas* is the reading of the sacred
classics under the roof of each householder. By this
means the family accumulate merit, and the longer
the reading is protracted the greater is the accumu-
lation. A twelve-volume book is taken in the houses
of the richer householders, each one of the twelve
or fifteen *lamas* taking a page, all reading at an
immense pace in a loud chant at the same time.
The reading of these volumes, which consist of
Buddhist metaphysics and philosophy, takes five
days, and while reading each *lama* has his *chang*
cup constantly replenished. In the poorer households
a classic of but one volume is taken, to lessen the
expense of feeding the *lamas*. Festivals and ceremonies follow each other closely until March, when

archery practice begins, and in April and May the people prepare for the operations of husbandry.

The weather in Kylang breaks in the middle of September, but so fascinating were the beauties and sublimity of Nature, and the virtues and culture of my Moravian friends, that, shutting my eyes to the possible perils of the Rotang, I remained until the harvest was brought home with joy and revelry, and the flush of autumn faded, and the first snows of winter gave an added majesty to the glorious valley. Then, reluctantly folding my tent, and taking the same faithful fellows who brought my baggage from Leh, I spent five weeks on the descent to the Panjāb, journeying through the paradise of Upper Kulu and the interesting native states of Mandi, Sukket, Bilaspur, and Bhaghat; and early in November reached the amenities and restraints of the civilisation of Simla.

THE END.

A CATALOG OF SELECTED
DOVER BOOKS
IN ALL FIELDS OF INTEREST

A CATALOG OF SELECTED DOVER
BOOKS IN ALL FIELDS OF INTEREST

CONCERNING THE SPIRITUAL IN ART, Wassily Kandinsky. Pioneering work by father of abstract art. Thoughts on color theory, nature of art. Analysis of earlier masters. 12 illustrations. 80pp. of text. 5⅜ x 8½. 23411-8

ANIMALS: 1,419 Copyright-Free Illustrations of Mammals, Birds, Fish, Insects, etc., Jim Harter (ed.). Clear wood engravings present, in extremely lifelike poses, over 1,000 species of animals. One of the most extensive pictorial sourcebooks of its kind. Captions. Index. 284pp. 9 x 12. 23766-4

CELTIC ART: The Methods of Construction, George Bain. Simple geometric techniques for making Celtic interlacements, spirals, Kells-type initials, animals, humans, etc. Over 500 illustrations. 160pp. 9 x 12. (Available in U.S. only.) 22923-8

AN ATLAS OF ANATOMY FOR ARTISTS, Fritz Schider. Most thorough reference work on art anatomy in the world. Hundreds of illustrations, including selections from works by Vesalius, Leonardo, Goya, Ingres, Michelangelo, others. 593 illustrations. 192pp. 7⅛ x 10¼. 20241-0

CELTIC HAND STROKE-BY-STROKE (Irish Half-Uncial from "The Book of Kells"): An Arthur Baker Calligraphy Manual, Arthur Baker. Complete guide to creating each letter of the alphabet in distinctive Celtic manner. Covers hand position, strokes, pens, inks, paper, more. Illustrated. 48pp. 8¼ x 11. 24336-2

EASY ORIGAMI, John Montroll. Charming collection of 32 projects (hat, cup, pelican, piano, swan, many more) specially designed for the novice origami hobbyist. Clearly illustrated easy-to-follow instructions insure that even beginning papercrafters will achieve successful results. 48pp. 8¼ x 11. 27298-2

THE COMPLETE BOOK OF BIRDHOUSE CONSTRUCTION FOR WOOD-WORKERS, Scott D. Campbell. Detailed instructions, illustrations, tables. Also data on bird habitat and instinct patterns. Bibliography. 3 tables. 63 illustrations in 15 figures. 48pp. 5¼ x 8½. 24407-5

BLOOMINGDALE'S ILLUSTRATED 1886 CATALOG: Fashions, Dry Goods and Housewares, Bloomingdale Brothers. Famed merchants' extremely rare catalog depicting about 1,700 products: clothing, housewares, firearms, dry goods, jewelry, more. Invaluable for dating, identifying vintage items. Also, copyright-free graphics for artists, designers. Co-published with Henry Ford Museum & Greenfield Village. 160pp. 8¼ x 11. 25780-0

HISTORIC COSTUME IN PICTURES, Braun & Schneider. Over 1,450 costumed figures in clearly detailed engravings–from dawn of civilization to end of 19th century. Captions. Many folk costumes. 256pp. 8⅜ x 11¾. 23150-X

STICKLEY CRAFTSMAN FURNITURE CATALOGS, Gustav Stickley and L. & J. G. Stickley. Beautiful, functional furniture in two authentic catalogs from 1910. 594 illustrations, including 277 photos, show settles, rockers, armchairs, reclining chairs, bookcases, desks, tables. 183pp. 6½ x 9¼. 23838-5

AMERICAN LOCOMOTIVES IN HISTORIC PHOTOGRAPHS: 1858 to 1949, Ron Ziel (ed.). A rare collection of 126 meticulously detailed official photographs, called "builder portraits," of American locomotives that majestically chronicle the rise of steam locomotive power in America. Introduction. Detailed captions. xi+ 129pp. 9 x 12. 27393-8

AMERICA'S LIGHTHOUSES: An Illustrated History, Francis Ross Holland, Jr. Delightfully written, profusely illustrated fact-filled survey of over 200 American lighthouses since 1716. History, anecdotes, technological advances, more. 240pp. 8 x 10¾. 25576-X

TOWARDS A NEW ARCHITECTURE, Le Corbusier. Pioneering manifesto by founder of "International School." Technical and aesthetic theories, views of industry, economics, relation of form to function, "mass-production split" and much more. Profusely illustrated. 320pp. 6⅛ x 9¼. (Available in U.S. only.) 25023-7

HOW THE OTHER HALF LIVES, Jacob Riis. Famous journalistic record, exposing poverty and degradation of New York slums around 1900, by major social reformer. 100 striking and influential photographs. 233pp. 10 x 7⅞. 22012-5

FRUIT KEY AND TWIG KEY TO TREES AND SHRUBS, William M. Harlow. One of the handiest and most widely used identification aids. Fruit key covers 120 deciduous and evergreen species; twig key 160 deciduous species. Easily used. Over 300 photographs. 126pp. 5⅜ x 8½. 20511-8

COMMON BIRD SONGS, Dr. Donald J. Borror. Songs of 60 most common U.S. birds: robins, sparrows, cardinals, bluejays, finches, more–arranged in order of increasing complexity. Up to 9 variations of songs of each species.
Cassette and manual 99911-4

ORCHIDS AS HOUSE PLANTS, Rebecca Tyson Northen. Grow cattleyas and many other kinds of orchids–in a window, in a case, or under artificial light. 63 illustrations. 148pp. 5⅜ x 8½. 23261-1

MONSTER MAZES, Dave Phillips. Masterful mazes at four levels of difficulty. Avoid deadly perils and evil creatures to find magical treasures. Solutions for all 32 exciting illustrated puzzles. 48pp. 8¼ x 11. 26005-4

MOZART'S DON GIOVANNI (DOVER OPERA LIBRETTO SERIES), Wolfgang Amadeus Mozart. Introduced and translated by Ellen H. Bleiler. Standard Italian libretto, with complete English translation. Convenient and thoroughly portable–an ideal companion for reading along with a recording or the performance itself. Introduction. List of characters. Plot summary. 121pp. 5¼ x 8½. 24944-1

TECHNICAL MANUAL AND DICTIONARY OF CLASSICAL BALLET, Gail Grant. Defines, explains, comments on steps, movements, poses and concepts. 15-page pictorial section. Basic book for student, viewer. 127pp. 5⅜ x 8½. 21843-0

THE CLARINET AND CLARINET PLAYING, David Pino. Lively, comprehensive work features suggestions about technique, musicianship, and musical interpretation, as well as guidelines for teaching, making your own reeds, and preparing for public performance. Includes an intriguing look at clarinet history. "A godsend," *The Clarinet,* Journal of the International Clarinet Society. Appendixes. 7 illus. 320pp. 5⅜ x 8½. 40270-3

HOLLYWOOD GLAMOR PORTRAITS, John Kobal (ed.). 145 photos from 1926-49. Harlow, Gable, Bogart, Bacall; 94 stars in all. Full background on photographers, technical aspects. 160pp. 8⅜ x 11¼. 23352-9

THE ANNOTATED CASEY AT THE BAT: A Collection of Ballads about the Mighty Casey/Third, Revised Edition, Martin Gardner (ed.). Amusing sequels and parodies of one of America's best-loved poems: Casey's Revenge, Why Casey Whiffed, Casey's Sister at the Bat, others. 256pp. 5⅜ x 8½. 28598-7

THE RAVEN AND OTHER FAVORITE POEMS, Edgar Allan Poe. Over 40 of the author's most memorable poems: "The Bells," "Ulalume," "Israfel," "To Helen," "The Conqueror Worm," "Eldorado," "Annabel Lee," many more. Alphabetic lists of titles and first lines. 64pp. 5$\frac{3}{16}$ x 8¼. 26685-0

PERSONAL MEMOIRS OF U. S. GRANT, Ulysses Simpson Grant. Intelligent, deeply moving firsthand account of Civil War campaigns, considered by many the finest military memoirs ever written. Includes letters, historic photographs, maps and more. 528pp. 6⅛ x 9¼. 28587-1

ANCIENT EGYPTIAN MATERIALS AND INDUSTRIES, A. Lucas and J. Harris. Fascinating, comprehensive, thoroughly documented text describes this ancient civilization's vast resources and the processes that incorporated them in daily life, including the use of animal products, building materials, cosmetics, perfumes and incense, fibers, glazed ware, glass and its manufacture, materials used in the mummification process, and much more. 544pp. 6⅛ x 9¼. (Available in U.S. only.) 40446-3

RUSSIAN STORIES/RUSSKIE RASSKAZY: A Dual-Language Book, edited by Gleb Struve. Twelve tales by such masters as Chekhov, Tolstoy, Dostoevsky, Pushkin, others. Excellent word-for-word English translations on facing pages, plus teaching and study aids, Russian/English vocabulary, biographical/critical introductions, more. 416pp. 5⅜ x 8½. 26244-8

PHILADELPHIA THEN AND NOW: 60 Sites Photographed in the Past and Present, Kenneth Finkel and Susan Oyama. Rare photographs of City Hall, Logan Square, Independence Hall, Betsy Ross House, other landmarks juxtaposed with contemporary views. Captures changing face of historic city. Introduction. Captions. 128pp. 8¼ x 11. 25790-8

AIA ARCHITECTURAL GUIDE TO NASSAU AND SUFFOLK COUNTIES, LONG ISLAND, The American Institute of Architects, Long Island Chapter, and the Society for the Preservation of Long Island Antiquities. Comprehensive, well-researched and generously illustrated volume brings to life over three centuries of Long Island's great architectural heritage. More than 240 photographs with authoritative, extensively detailed captions. 176pp. 8¼ x 11. 26946-9

NORTH AMERICAN INDIAN LIFE: Customs and Traditions of 23 Tribes, Elsie Clews Parsons (ed.). 27 fictionalized essays by noted anthropologists examine religion, customs, government, additional facets of life among the Winnebago, Crow, Zuni, Eskimo, other tribes. 480pp. 6⅛ x 9¼. 27377-6

FRANK LLOYD WRIGHT'S DANA HOUSE, Donald Hoffmann. Pictorial essay of residential masterpiece with over 160 interior and exterior photos, plans, elevations, sketches and studies. 128pp. 9¼ x 10¾.   29120-0

THE MALE AND FEMALE FIGURE IN MOTION: 60 Classic Photographic Sequences, Eadweard Muybridge. 60 true-action photographs of men and women walking, running, climbing, bending, turning, etc., reproduced from rare 19th-century masterpiece. vi + 121pp. 9 x 12.   24745-7

1001 QUESTIONS ANSWERED ABOUT THE SEASHORE, N. J. Berrill and Jacquelyn Berrill. Queries answered about dolphins, sea snails, sponges, starfish, fishes, shore birds, many others. Covers appearance, breeding, growth, feeding, much more. 305pp. 5¼ x 8¼.   23366-9

ATTRACTING BIRDS TO YOUR YARD, William J. Weber. Easy-to-follow guide offers advice on how to attract the greatest diversity of birds: birdhouses, feeders, water and waterers, much more. 96pp. 5³⁄₁₆ x 8¼.   28927-3

MEDICINAL AND OTHER USES OF NORTH AMERICAN PLANTS: A Historical Survey with Special Reference to the Eastern Indian Tribes, Charlotte Erichsen-Brown. Chronological historical citations document 500 years of usage of plants, trees, shrubs native to eastern Canada, northeastern U.S. Also complete identifying information. 343 illustrations. 544pp. 6½ x 9¼.   25951-X

STORYBOOK MAZES, Dave Phillips. 23 stories and mazes on two-page spreads: Wizard of Oz, Treasure Island, Robin Hood, etc. Solutions. 64pp. 8¼ x 11. 23628-5

AMERICAN NEGRO SONGS: 230 Folk Songs and Spirituals, Religious and Secular, John W. Work. This authoritative study traces the African influences of songs sung and played by black Americans at work, in church, and as entertainment. The author discusses the lyric significance of such songs as "Swing Low, Sweet Chariot," "John Henry," and others and offers the words and music for 230 songs. Bibliography. Index of Song Titles. 272pp. 6½ x 9¼.   40271-1

MOVIE-STAR PORTRAITS OF THE FORTIES, John Kobal (ed.). 163 glamor, studio photos of 106 stars of the 1940s: Rita Hayworth, Ava Gardner, Marlon Brando, Clark Gable, many more. 176pp. 8⅜ x 11¼.   23546-7

BENCHLEY LOST AND FOUND, Robert Benchley. Finest humor from early 30s, about pet peeves, child psychologists, post office and others. Mostly unavailable elsewhere. 73 illustrations by Peter Arno and others. 183pp. 5⅜ x 8½.   22410-4

YEKL and THE IMPORTED BRIDEGROOM AND OTHER STORIES OF YIDDISH NEW YORK, Abraham Cahan. Film Hester Street based on *Yekl* (1896). Novel, other stories among first about Jewish immigrants on N.Y.'s East Side. 240pp. 5⅜ x 8½.   22427-9

SELECTED POEMS, Walt Whitman. Generous sampling from *Leaves of Grass*. Twenty-four poems include "I Hear America Singing," "Song of the Open Road," "I Sing the Body Electric," "When Lilacs Last in the Dooryard Bloom'd," "O Captain! My Captain!"–all reprinted from an authoritative edition. Lists of titles and first lines. 128pp. 5³⁄₁₆ x 8¼.   26878-0

THE BEST TALES OF HOFFMANN, E. T. A. Hoffmann. 10 of Hoffmann's most important stories: "Nutcracker and the King of Mice," "The Golden Flowerpot," etc. 458pp. 5⅜ x 8½. 21793-0

FROM FETISH TO GOD IN ANCIENT EGYPT, E. A. Wallis Budge. Rich detailed survey of Egyptian conception of "God" and gods, magic, cult of animals, Osiris, more. Also, superb English translations of hymns and legends. 240 illustrations. 545pp. 5⅜ x 8½. 25803-3

FRENCH STORIES/CONTES FRANÇAIS: A Dual-Language Book, Wallace Fowlie. Ten stories by French masters, Voltaire to Camus: "Micromegas" by Voltaire; "The Atheist's Mass" by Balzac; "Minuet" by de Maupassant; "The Guest" by Camus, six more. Excellent English translations on facing pages. Also French-English vocabulary list, exercises, more. 352pp. 5⅜ x 8½. 26443-2

CHICAGO AT THE TURN OF THE CENTURY IN PHOTOGRAPHS: 122 Historic Views from the Collections of the Chicago Historical Society, Larry A. Viskochil. Rare large-format prints offer detailed views of City Hall, State Street, the Loop, Hull House, Union Station, many other landmarks, circa 1904-1913. Introduction. Captions. Maps. 144pp. 9⅜ x 12¼. 24656-6

OLD BROOKLYN IN EARLY PHOTOGRAPHS, 1865-1929, William Lee Younger. Luna Park, Gravesend race track, construction of Grand Army Plaza, moving of Hotel Brighton, etc. 157 previously unpublished photographs. 165pp. 8⅞ x 11¾. 23587-4

THE MYTHS OF THE NORTH AMERICAN INDIANS, Lewis Spence. Rich anthology of the myths and legends of the Algonquins, Iroquois, Pawnees and Sioux, prefaced by an extensive historical and ethnological commentary. 36 illustrations. 480pp. 5⅜ x 8½. 25967-6

AN ENCYCLOPEDIA OF BATTLES: Accounts of Over 1,560 Battles from 1479 B.C. to the Present, David Eggenberger. Essential details of every major battle in recorded history from the first battle of Megiddo in 1479 B.C. to Grenada in 1984. List of Battle Maps. New Appendix covering the years 1967-1984. Index. 99 illustrations. 544pp. 6½ x 9¼. 24913-1

SAILING ALONE AROUND THE WORLD, Captain Joshua Slocum. First man to sail around the world, alone, in small boat. One of great feats of seamanship told in delightful manner. 67 illustrations. 294pp. 5⅜ x 8½. 20326-3

ANARCHISM AND OTHER ESSAYS, Emma Goldman. Powerful, penetrating, prophetic essays on direct action, role of minorities, prison reform, puritan hypocrisy, violence, etc. 271pp. 5⅜ x 8½. 22484-8

MYTHS OF THE HINDUS AND BUDDHISTS, Ananda K. Coomaraswamy and Sister Nivedita. Great stories of the epics; deeds of Krishna, Shiva, taken from puranas, Vedas, folk tales; etc. 32 illustrations. 400pp. 5⅜ x 8½. 21759-0

THE TRAUMA OF BIRTH, Otto Rank. Rank's controversial thesis that anxiety neurosis is caused by profound psychological trauma which occurs at birth. 256pp. 5⅜ x 8½. 27974-X

A THEOLOGICO-POLITICAL TREATISE, Benedict Spinoza. Also contains unfinished Political Treatise. Great classic on religious liberty, theory of government on common consent. R. Elwes translation. Total of 421pp. 5⅜ x 8½. 20249-6

MY BONDAGE AND MY FREEDOM, Frederick Douglass. Born a slave, Douglass became outspoken force in antislavery movement. The best of Douglass' autobiographies. Graphic description of slave life. 464pp. 5⅜ x 8½.   22457-0

FOLLOWING THE EQUATOR: A Journey Around the World, Mark Twain. Fascinating humorous account of 1897 voyage to Hawaii, Australia, India, New Zealand, etc. Ironic, bemused reports on peoples, customs, climate, flora and fauna, politics, much more. 197 illustrations. 720pp. 5⅜ x 8½.   26113-1

THE PEOPLE CALLED SHAKERS, Edward D. Andrews. Definitive study of Shakers: origins, beliefs, practices, dances, social organization, furniture and crafts, etc. 33 illustrations. 351pp. 5⅜ x 8½.   21081-2

THE MYTHS OF GREECE AND ROME, H. A. Guerber. A classic of mythology, generously illustrated, long prized for its simple, graphic, accurate retelling of the principal myths of Greece and Rome, and for its commentary on their origins and significance. With 64 illustrations by Michelangelo, Raphael, Titian, Rubens, Canova, Bernini and others. 480pp. 5⅜ x 8½.   27584-1

PSYCHOLOGY OF MUSIC, Carl E. Seashore. Classic work discusses music as a medium from psychological viewpoint. Clear treatment of physical acoustics, auditory apparatus, sound perception, development of musical skills, nature of musical feeling, host of other topics. 88 figures. 408pp. 5⅜ x 8½.   21851-1

THE PHILOSOPHY OF HISTORY, Georg W. Hegel. Great classic of Western thought develops concept that history is not chance but rational process, the evolution of freedom. 457pp. 5⅜ x 8½.   20112-0

THE BOOK OF TEA, Kakuzo Okakura. Minor classic of the Orient: entertaining, charming explanation, interpretation of traditional Japanese culture in terms of tea ceremony. 94pp. 5⅜ x 8½.   20070-1

LIFE IN ANCIENT EGYPT, Adolf Erman. Fullest, most thorough, detailed older account with much not in more recent books, domestic life, religion, magic, medicine, commerce, much more. Many illustrations reproduce tomb paintings, carvings, hieroglyphs, etc. 597pp. 5⅜ x 8½.   22632-8

SUNDIALS, Their Theory and Construction, Albert Waugh. Far and away the best, most thorough coverage of ideas, mathematics concerned, types, construction, adjusting anywhere. Simple, nontechnical treatment allows even children to build several of these dials. Over 100 illustrations. 230pp. 5⅜ x 8½.   22947-5

THEORETICAL HYDRODYNAMICS, L. M. Milne-Thomson. Classic exposition of the mathematical theory of fluid motion, applicable to both hydrodynamics and aerodynamics. Over 600 exercises. 768pp. 6⅛ x 9¼.   68970-0

SONGS OF EXPERIENCE: Facsimile Reproduction with 26 Plates in Full Color, William Blake. 26 full-color plates from a rare 1826 edition. Includes "The Tyger," "London," "Holy Thursday," and other poems. Printed text of poems. 48pp. 5¼ x 7.   24636-1

OLD-TIME VIGNETTES IN FULL COLOR, Carol Belanger Grafton (ed.). Over 390 charming, often sentimental illustrations, selected from archives of Victorian graphics—pretty women posing, children playing, food, flowers, kittens and puppies, smiling cherubs, birds and butterflies, much more. All copyright-free. 48pp. 9¼ x 12¼.   27269-9

PERSPECTIVE FOR ARTISTS, Rex Vicat Cole. Depth, perspective of sky and sea, shadows, much more, not usually covered. 391 diagrams, 81 reproductions of drawings and paintings. 279pp. 5⅜ x 8½. 22487-2

DRAWING THE LIVING FIGURE, Joseph Sheppard. Innovative approach to artistic anatomy focuses on specifics of surface anatomy, rather than muscles and bones. Over 170 drawings of live models in front, back and side views, and in widely varying poses. Accompanying diagrams. 177 illustrations. Introduction. Index. 144pp. 8⅜ x11¼. 26723-7

GOTHIC AND OLD ENGLISH ALPHABETS: 100 Complete Fonts, Dan X. Solo. Add power, elegance to posters, signs, other graphics with 100 stunning copyright-free alphabets: Blackstone, Dolbey, Germania, 97 more–including many lower-case, numerals, punctuation marks. 104pp. 8⅛ x 11. 24695-7

HOW TO DO BEADWORK, Mary White. Fundamental book on craft from simple projects to five-bead chains and woven works. 106 illustrations. 142pp. 5⅜ x 8. 20697-1

THE BOOK OF WOOD CARVING, Charles Marshall Sayers. Finest book for beginners discusses fundamentals and offers 34 designs. "Absolutely first rate . . . well thought out and well executed."–E. J. Tangerman. 118pp. 7¾ x 10⅝. 23654-4

ILLUSTRATED CATALOG OF CIVIL WAR MILITARY GOODS: Union Army Weapons, Insignia, Uniform Accessories, and Other Equipment, Schuyler, Hartley, and Graham. Rare, profusely illustrated 1846 catalog includes Union Army uniform and dress regulations, arms and ammunition, coats, insignia, flags, swords, rifles, etc. 226 illustrations. 160pp. 9 x 12. 24939-5

WOMEN'S FASHIONS OF THE EARLY 1900s: An Unabridged Republication of "New York Fashions, 1909," National Cloak & Suit Co. Rare catalog of mail-order fashions documents women's and children's clothing styles shortly after the turn of the century. Captions offer full descriptions, prices. Invaluable resource for fashion, costume historians. Approximately 725 illustrations. 128pp. 8⅜ x 11¼. 27276-1

THE 1912 AND 1915 GUSTAV STICKLEY FURNITURE CATALOGS, Gustav Stickley. With over 200 detailed illustrations and descriptions, these two catalogs are essential reading and reference materials and identification guides for Stickley furniture. Captions cite materials, dimensions and prices. 112pp. 6½ x 9¼. 26676-1

EARLY AMERICAN LOCOMOTIVES, John H. White, Jr. Finest locomotive engravings from early 19th century: historical (1804–74), main-line (after 1870), special, foreign, etc. 147 plates. 142pp. 11⅜ x 8¼. 22772-3

THE TALL SHIPS OF TODAY IN PHOTOGRAPHS, Frank O. Braynard. Lavishly illustrated tribute to nearly 100 majestic contemporary sailing vessels: Amerigo Vespucci, Clearwater, Constitution, Eagle, Mayflower, Sea Cloud, Victory, many more. Authoritative captions provide statistics, background on each ship. 190 black-and-white photographs and illustrations. Introduction. 128pp. 8⅞ x 11¾. 27163-3

LITTLE BOOK OF EARLY AMERICAN CRAFTS AND TRADES, Peter Stockham (ed.). 1807 children's book explains crafts and trades: baker, hatter, cooper, potter, and many others. 23 copperplate illustrations. 140pp. 4⅝ x 6. 23336-7

VICTORIAN FASHIONS AND COSTUMES FROM HARPER'S BAZAR, 1867–1898, Stella Blum (ed.). Day costumes, evening wear, sports clothes, shoes, hats, other accessories in over 1,000 detailed engravings. 320pp. 9⅜ x 12¼. 22990-4

GUSTAV STICKLEY, THE CRAFTSMAN, Mary Ann Smith. Superb study surveys broad scope of Stickley's achievement, especially in architecture. Design philosophy, rise and fall of the Craftsman empire, descriptions and floor plans for many Craftsman houses, more. 86 black-and-white halftones. 31 line illustrations. Introduction 208pp. 6½ x 9¼. 27210-9

THE LONG ISLAND RAIL ROAD IN EARLY PHOTOGRAPHS, Ron Ziel. Over 220 rare photos, informative text document origin (1844) and development of rail service on Long Island. Vintage views of early trains, locomotives, stations, passengers, crews, much more. Captions. 8⅞ x 11¾. 26301-0

VOYAGE OF THE LIBERDADE, Joshua Slocum. Great 19th-century mariner's thrilling, first-hand account of the wreck of his ship off South America, the 35-foot boat he built from the wreckage, and its remarkable voyage home. 128pp. 5⅜ x 8½. 40022-0

TEN BOOKS ON ARCHITECTURE, Vitruvius. The most important book ever written on architecture. Early Roman aesthetics, technology, classical orders, site selection, all other aspects. Morgan translation. 331pp. 5⅜ x 8½. 20645-9

THE HUMAN FIGURE IN MOTION, Eadweard Muybridge. More than 4,500 stopped-action photos, in action series, showing undraped men, women, children jumping, lying down, throwing, sitting, wrestling, carrying, etc. 390pp. 7⅞ x 10⅝. 20204-6 Clothbd.

TREES OF THE EASTERN AND CENTRAL UNITED STATES AND CANADA, William M. Harlow. Best one-volume guide to 140 trees. Full descriptions, woodlore, range, etc. Over 600 illustrations. Handy size. 288pp. 4½ x 6⅜. 20395-6

SONGS OF WESTERN BIRDS, Dr. Donald J. Borror. Complete song and call repertoire of 60 western species, including flycatchers, juncoes, cactus wrens, many more–includes fully illustrated booklet. Cassette and manual 99913-0

GROWING AND USING HERBS AND SPICES, Milo Miloradovich. Versatile handbook provides all the information needed for cultivation and use of all the herbs and spices available in North America. 4 illustrations. Index. Glossary. 236pp. 5⅜ x 8½. 25058-X

BIG BOOK OF MAZES AND LABYRINTHS, Walter Shepherd. 50 mazes and labyrinths in all–classical, solid, ripple, and more–in one great volume. Perfect inexpensive puzzler for clever youngsters. Full solutions. 112pp. 8⅛ x 11. 22951-3

PIANO TUNING, J. Cree Fischer. Clearest, best book for beginner, amateur. Simple repairs, raising dropped notes, tuning by easy method of flattened fifths. No previous skills needed. 4 illustrations. 201pp. 5⅜ x 8½. 23267-0

HINTS TO SINGERS, Lillian Nordica. Selecting the right teacher, developing confidence, overcoming stage fright, and many other important skills receive thoughtful discussion in this indispensible guide, written by a world-famous diva of four decades' experience. 96pp. 5⅜ x 8½. 40094-8

THE COMPLETE NONSENSE OF EDWARD LEAR, Edward Lear. All nonsense limericks, zany alphabets, Owl and Pussycat, songs, nonsense botany, etc., illustrated by Lear. Total of 320pp. 5⅜ x 8½. (Available in U.S. only.) 20167-8

VICTORIAN PARLOUR POETRY: An Annotated Anthology, Michael R. Turner. 117 gems by Longfellow, Tennyson, Browning, many lesser-known poets. "The Village Blacksmith," "Curfew Must Not Ring Tonight," "Only a Baby Small," dozens more, often difficult to find elsewhere. Index of poets, titles, first lines. xxiii + 325pp. 5⅝ x 8¼. 27044-0

DUBLINERS, James Joyce. Fifteen stories offer vivid, tightly focused observations of the lives of Dublin's poorer classes. At least one, "The Dead," is considered a masterpiece. Reprinted complete and unabridged from standard edition. 160pp. 5$\frac{3}{16}$ x 8¼. 26870-5

GREAT WEIRD TALES: 14 Stories by Lovecraft, Blackwood, Machen and Others, S. T. Joshi (ed.). 14 spellbinding tales, including "The Sin Eater," by Fiona McLeod, "The Eye Above the Mantel," by Frank Belknap Long, as well as renowned works by R. H. Barlow, Lord Dunsany, Arthur Machen, W. C. Morrow and eight other masters of the genre. 256pp. 5⅜ x 8½. (Available in U.S. only.) 40436-6

THE BOOK OF THE SACRED MAGIC OF ABRAMELIN THE MAGE, translated by S. MacGregor Mathers. Medieval manuscript of ceremonial magic. Basic document in Aleister Crowley, Golden Dawn groups. 268pp. 5⅜ x 8½. 23211-5

NEW RUSSIAN-ENGLISH AND ENGLISH-RUSSIAN DICTIONARY, M. A. O'Brien. This is a remarkably handy Russian dictionary, containing a surprising amount of information, including over 70,000 entries. 366pp. 4½ x 6⅛. 20208-9

HISTORIC HOMES OF THE AMERICAN PRESIDENTS, Second, Revised Edition, Irvin Haas. A traveler's guide to American Presidential homes, most open to the public, depicting and describing homes occupied by every American President from George Washington to George Bush. With visiting hours, admission charges, travel routes. 175 photographs. Index. 160pp. 8¼ x 11. 26751-2

NEW YORK IN THE FORTIES, Andreas Feininger. 162 brilliant photographs by the well-known photographer, formerly with *Life* magazine. Commuters, shoppers, Times Square at night, much else from city at its peak. Captions by John von Hartz. 181pp. 9¼ x 10¾. 23585-8

INDIAN SIGN LANGUAGE, William Tomkins. Over 525 signs developed by Sioux and other tribes. Written instructions and diagrams. Also 290 pictographs. 111pp. 6⅛ x 9¼. 22029-X

ANATOMY: A Complete Guide for Artists, Joseph Sheppard. A master of figure drawing shows artists how to render human anatomy convincingly. Over 460 illustrations. 224pp. 8⅜ x 11¼. 27279-6

MEDIEVAL CALLIGRAPHY: Its History and Technique, Marc Drogin. Spirited history, comprehensive instruction manual covers 13 styles (ca. 4th century through 15th). Excellent photographs; directions for duplicating medieval techniques with modern tools. 224pp. 8⅜ x 11¼. 26142-5

DRIED FLOWERS: How to Prepare Them, Sarah Whitlock and Martha Rankin. Complete instructions on how to use silica gel, meal and borax, perlite aggregate, sand and borax, glycerine and water to create attractive permanent flower arrangements. 12 illustrations. 32pp. 5⅜ x 8½. 21802-3

EASY-TO-MAKE BIRD FEEDERS FOR WOODWORKERS, Scott D. Campbell. Detailed, simple-to-use guide for designing, constructing, caring for and using feeders. Text, illustrations for 12 classic and contemporary designs. 96pp. 5⅜ x 8½. 25847-5

SCOTTISH WONDER TALES FROM MYTH AND LEGEND, Donald A. Mackenzie. 16 lively tales tell of giants rumbling down mountainsides, of a magic wand that turns stone pillars into warriors, of gods and goddesses, evil hags, powerful forces and more. 240pp. 5⅜ x 8½. 29677-6

THE HISTORY OF UNDERCLOTHES, C. Willett Cunnington and Phyllis Cunnington. Fascinating, well-documented survey covering six centuries of English undergarments, enhanced with over 100 illustrations: 12th-century laced-up bodice, footed long drawers (1795), 19th-century bustles, 19th-century corsets for men, Victorian "bust improvers," much more. 272pp. 5⅜ x 8¼. 27124-2

ARTS AND CRAFTS FURNITURE: The Complete Brooks Catalog of 1912, Brooks Manufacturing Co. Photos and detailed descriptions of more than 150 now very collectible furniture designs from the Arts and Crafts movement depict davenports, settees, buffets, desks, tables, chairs, bedsteads, dressers and more, all built of solid, quarter-sawed oak. Invaluable for students and enthusiasts of antiques, Americana and the decorative arts. 80pp. 6½ x 9¼. 27471-3

WILBUR AND ORVILLE: A Biography of the Wright Brothers, Fred Howard. Definitive, crisply written study tells the full story of the brothers' lives and work. A vividly written biography, unparalleled in scope and color, that also captures the spirit of an extraordinary era. 560pp. 6⅛ x 9¼. 40297-5

THE ARTS OF THE SAILOR: Knotting, Splicing and Ropework, Hervey Garrett Smith. Indispensable shipboard reference covers tools, basic knots and useful hitches; handsewing and canvas work, more. Over 100 illustrations. Delightful reading for sea lovers. 256pp. 5⅜ x 8½. 26440-8

FRANK LLOYD WRIGHT'S FALLINGWATER: The House and Its History, Second, Revised Edition, Donald Hoffmann. A total revision–both in text and illustrations–of the standard document on Fallingwater, the boldest, most personal architectural statement of Wright's mature years, updated with valuable new material from the recently opened Frank Lloyd Wright Archives. "Fascinating"–*The New York Times*. 116 illustrations. 128pp. 9¼ x 10¾. 27430-6

PHOTOGRAPHIC SKETCHBOOK OF THE CIVIL WAR, Alexander Gardner. 100 photos taken on field during the Civil War. Famous shots of Manassas Harper's Ferry, Lincoln, Richmond, slave pens, etc. 244pp. 10⅝ x 8¼. 22731-6

FIVE ACRES AND INDEPENDENCE, Maurice G. Kains. Great back-to-the-land classic explains basics of self-sufficient farming. The one book to get. 95 illustrations. 397pp. 5⅜ x 8½. 20974-1

SONGS OF EASTERN BIRDS, Dr. Donald J. Borror. Songs and calls of 60 species most common to eastern U.S.: warblers, woodpeckers, flycatchers, thrushes, larks, many more in high-quality recording. Cassette and manual 99912-2

A MODERN HERBAL, Margaret Grieve. Much the fullest, most exact, most useful compilation of herbal material. Gigantic alphabetical encyclopedia, from aconite to zedoary, gives botanical information, medical properties, folklore, economic uses, much else. Indispensable to serious reader. 161 illustrations. 888pp. 6½ x 9¼. 2-vol. set. (Available in U.S. only.) Vol. I: 22798-7
Vol. II: 22799-5

HIDDEN TREASURE MAZE BOOK, Dave Phillips. Solve 34 challenging mazes accompanied by heroic tales of adventure. Evil dragons, people-eating plants, blood-thirsty giants, many more dangerous adversaries lurk at every twist and turn. 34 mazes, stories, solutions. 48pp. 8¼ x 11. 24566-7

LETTERS OF W. A. MOZART, Wolfgang A. Mozart. Remarkable letters show bawdy wit, humor, imagination, musical insights, contemporary musical world; includes some letters from Leopold Mozart. 276pp. 5⅜ x 8½. 22859-2

BASIC PRINCIPLES OF CLASSICAL BALLET, Agrippina Vaganova. Great Russian theoretician, teacher explains methods for teaching classical ballet. 118 illustrations. 175pp. 5⅜ x 8½. 22036-2

THE JUMPING FROG, Mark Twain. Revenge edition. The original story of The Celebrated Jumping Frog of Calaveras County, a hapless French translation, and Twain's hilarious "retranslation" from the French. 12 illustrations. 66pp. 5⅜ x 8½. 22686-7

BEST REMEMBERED POEMS, Martin Gardner (ed.). The 126 poems in this superb collection of 19th- and 20th-century British and American verse range from Shelley's "To a Skylark" to the impassioned "Renascence" of Edna St. Vincent Millay and to Edward Lear's whimsical "The Owl and the Pussycat." 224pp. 5⅜ x 8½. 27165-X

COMPLETE SONNETS, William Shakespeare. Over 150 exquisite poems deal with love, friendship, the tyranny of time, beauty's evanescence, death and other themes in language of remarkable power, precision and beauty. Glossary of archaic terms. 80pp. 5³⁄₁₆ x 8¼. 26686-9

THE BATTLES THAT CHANGED HISTORY, Fletcher Pratt. Eminent historian profiles 16 crucial conflicts, ancient to modern, that changed the course of civilization. 352pp. 5⅜ x 8½. 41129-X

THE WIT AND HUMOR OF OSCAR WILDE, Alvin Redman (ed.). More than 1,000 ripostes, paradoxes, wisecracks: Work is the curse of the drinking classes; I can resist everything except temptation; etc. 258pp. 5⅜ x 8½. 20602-5

SHAKESPEARE LEXICON AND QUOTATION DICTIONARY, Alexander Schmidt. Full definitions, locations, shades of meaning in every word in plays and poems. More than 50,000 exact quotations. 1,485pp. 6½ x 9¼. 2-vol. set.
Vol. 1: 22726-X
Vol. 2: 22727-8

SELECTED POEMS, Emily Dickinson. Over 100 best-known, best-loved poems by one of America's foremost poets, reprinted from authoritative early editions. No comparable edition at this price. Index of first lines. 64pp. 5³⁄₁₆ x 8¼. 26466-1

THE INSIDIOUS DR. FU-MANCHU, Sax Rohmer. The first of the popular mystery series introduces a pair of English detectives to their archnemesis, the diabolical Dr. Fu-Manchu. Flavorful atmosphere, fast-paced action, and colorful characters enliven this classic of the genre. 208pp. 5³⁄₁₆ x 8¼. 29898-1

THE MALLEUS MALEFICARUM OF KRAMER AND SPRENGER, translated by Montague Summers. Full text of most important witchhunter's "bible," used by both Catholics and Protestants. 278pp. 6⅝ x 10. 22802-9

SPANISH STORIES/CUENTOS ESPAÑOLES: A Dual-Language Book, Angel Flores (ed.). Unique format offers 13 great stories in Spanish by Cervantes, Borges, others. Faithful English translations on facing pages. 352pp. 5⅜ x 8½. 25399-6

GARDEN CITY, LONG ISLAND, IN EARLY PHOTOGRAPHS, 1869–1919, Mildred H. Smith. Handsome treasury of 118 vintage pictures, accompanied by carefully researched captions, document the Garden City Hotel fire (1899), the Vanderbilt Cup Race (1908), the first airmail flight departing from the Nassau Boulevard Aerodrome (1911), and much more. 96pp. 8⅞ x 11¾. 40669-5

OLD QUEENS, N.Y., IN EARLY PHOTOGRAPHS, Vincent F. Seyfried and William Asadorian. Over 160 rare photographs of Maspeth, Jamaica, Jackson Heights, and other areas. Vintage views of DeWitt Clinton mansion, 1939 World's Fair and more. Captions. 192pp. 8⅞ x 11. 26358-4

CAPTURED BY THE INDIANS: 15 Firsthand Accounts, 1750-1870, Frederick Drimmer. Astounding true historical accounts of grisly torture, bloody conflicts, relentless pursuits, miraculous escapes and more, by people who lived to tell the tale. 384pp. 5⅜ x 8½. 24901-8

THE WORLD'S GREAT SPEECHES (Fourth Enlarged Edition), Lewis Copeland, Lawrence W. Lamm, and Stephen J. McKenna. Nearly 300 speeches provide public speakers with a wealth of updated quotes and inspiration–from Pericles' funeral oration and William Jennings Bryan's "Cross of Gold Speech" to Malcolm X's powerful words on the Black Revolution and Earl of Spenser's tribute to his sister, Diana, Princess of Wales. 944pp. 5⅜ x 8⅜. 40903-1

THE BOOK OF THE SWORD, Sir Richard F. Burton. Great Victorian scholar/adventurer's eloquent, erudite history of the "queen of weapons"–from prehistory to early Roman Empire. Evolution and development of early swords, variations (sabre, broadsword, cutlass, scimitar, etc.), much more. 336pp. 6⅛ x 9¼.
25434-8

AUTOBIOGRAPHY: The Story of My Experiments with Truth, Mohandas K. Gandhi. Boyhood, legal studies, purification, the growth of the Satyagraha (nonviolent protest) movement. Critical, inspiring work of the man responsible for the freedom of India. 480pp. 5⅜ x 8½. (Available in U.S. only.) 24593-4

CELTIC MYTHS AND LEGENDS, T. W. Rolleston. Masterful retelling of Irish and Welsh stories and tales. Cuchulain, King Arthur, Deirdre, the Grail, many more. First paperback edition. 58 full-page illustrations. 512pp. 5⅜ x 8½. 26507-2

THE PRINCIPLES OF PSYCHOLOGY, William James. Famous long course complete, unabridged. Stream of thought, time perception, memory, experimental methods; great work decades ahead of its time. 94 figures. 1,391pp. 5⅜ x 8½. 2-vol. set.
Vol. I: 20381-6   Vol. II: 20382-4

THE WORLD AS WILL AND REPRESENTATION, Arthur Schopenhauer. Definitive English translation of Schopenhauer's life work, correcting more than 1,000 errors, omissions in earlier translations. Translated by E. F. J. Payne. Total of 1,269pp. 5⅜ x 8½. 2-vol. set.
Vol. 1: 21761-2   Vol. 2: 21762-0

MAGIC AND MYSTERY IN TIBET, Madame Alexandra David-Neel. Experiences among lamas, magicians, sages, sorcerers, Bonpa wizards. A true psychic discovery. 32 illustrations. 321pp. 5⅜ x 8½. (Available in U.S. only.) 22682-4

THE EGYPTIAN BOOK OF THE DEAD, E. A. Wallis Budge. Complete reproduction of Ani's papyrus, finest ever found. Full hieroglyphic text, interlinear transliteration, word-for-word translation, smooth translation. 533pp. 6½ x 9¼. 21866-X

MATHEMATICS FOR THE NONMATHEMATICIAN, Morris Kline. Detailed, college-level treatment of mathematics in cultural and historical context, with numerous exercises. Recommended Reading Lists. Tables. Numerous figures. 641pp. 5⅜ x 8½. 24823-2

PROBABILISTIC METHODS IN THE THEORY OF STRUCTURES, Isaac Elishakoff. Well-written introduction covers the elements of the theory of probability from two or more random variables, the reliability of such multivariable structures, the theory of random function, Monte Carlo methods of treating problems incapable of exact solution, and more. Examples. 502pp. 5⅜ x 8½. 40691-1

THE RIME OF THE ANCIENT MARINER, Gustave Doré, S. T. Coleridge. Doré's finest work; 34 plates capture moods, subtleties of poem. Flawless full-size reproductions printed on facing pages with authoritative text of poem. "Beautiful. Simply beautiful."–*Publisher's Weekly.* 77pp. 9¼ x 12. 22305-1

NORTH AMERICAN INDIAN DESIGNS FOR ARTISTS AND CRAFTSPEOPLE, Eva Wilson. Over 360 authentic copyright-free designs adapted from Navajo blankets, Hopi pottery, Sioux buffalo hides, more. Geometrics, symbolic figures, plant and animal motifs, etc. 128pp. 8⅜ x 11. (Not for sale in the United Kingdom.) 25341-4

SCULPTURE: Principles and Practice, Louis Slobodkin. Step-by-step approach to clay, plaster, metals, stone; classical and modern. 253 drawings, photos. 255pp. 8⅛ x 11. 22960-2

THE INFLUENCE OF SEA POWER UPON HISTORY, 1660–1783, A. T. Mahan. Influential classic of naval history and tactics still used as text in war colleges. First paperback edition. 4 maps. 24 battle plans. 640pp. 5⅜ x 8½. 25509-3

THE STORY OF THE TITANIC AS TOLD BY ITS SURVIVORS, Jack Winocour (ed.). What it was really like. Panic, despair, shocking inefficiency, and a little heroism. More thrilling than any fictional account. 26 illustrations. 320pp. 5⅜ x 8½.
20610-6

FAIRY AND FOLK TALES OF THE IRISH PEASANTRY, William Butler Yeats (ed.). Treasury of 64 tales from the twilight world of Celtic myth and legend: "The Soul Cages," "The Kildare Pooka," "King O'Toole and his Goose," many more. Introduction and Notes by W. B. Yeats. 352pp. 5⅜ x 8½.
26941-8

BUDDHIST MAHAYANA TEXTS, E. B. Cowell and others (eds.). Superb, accurate translations of basic documents in Mahayana Buddhism, highly important in history of religions. The Buddha-karita of Asvaghosha, Larger Sukhavativyuha, more. 448pp. 5⅜ x 8½.
25552-2

ONE TWO THREE . . . INFINITY: Facts and Speculations of Science, George Gamow. Great physicist's fascinating, readable overview of contemporary science: number theory, relativity, fourth dimension, entropy, genes, atomic structure, much more. 128 illustrations. Index. 352pp. 5⅜ x 8½.
25664-2

EXPERIMENTATION AND MEASUREMENT, W. J. Youden. Introductory manual explains laws of measurement in simple terms and offers tips for achieving accuracy and minimizing errors. Mathematics of measurement, use of instruments, experimenting with machines. 1994 edition. Foreword. Preface. Introduction. Epilogue. Selected Readings. Glossary. Index. Tables and figures. 128pp. 5⅜ x 8½.
40451-X

DALÍ ON MODERN ART: The Cuckolds of Antiquated Modern Art, Salvador Dalí. Influential painter skewers modern art and its practitioners. Outrageous evaluations of Picasso, Cézanne, Turner, more. 15 renderings of paintings discussed. 44 calligraphic decorations by Dalí. 96pp. 5⅜ x 8½. (Available in U.S. only.)
29220-7

ANTIQUE PLAYING CARDS: A Pictorial History, Henry René D'Allemagne. Over 900 elaborate, decorative images from rare playing cards (14th–20th centuries): Bacchus, death, dancing dogs, hunting scenes, royal coats of arms, players cheating, much more. 96pp. 9¼ x 12¼.
29265-7

MAKING FURNITURE MASTERPIECES: 30 Projects with Measured Drawings, Franklin H. Gottshall. Step-by-step instructions, illustrations for constructing handsome, useful pieces, among them a Sheraton desk, Chippendale chair, Spanish desk, Queen Anne table and a William and Mary dressing mirror. 224pp. 8⅛ x 11¼.
29338-6

THE FOSSIL BOOK: A Record of Prehistoric Life, Patricia V. Rich et al. Profusely illustrated definitive guide covers everything from single-celled organisms and dinosaurs to birds and mammals and the interplay between climate and man. Over 1,500 illustrations. 760pp. 7½ x 10⅛.
29371-8